Warrior • 24

Austrian Grenadiers and Infantry 1788–1816

David Hollins · Illustrated by Jeffrey Burn

First published in Great Britain in 1998 by Osprey Publishing,
Midland House, West Way, Botley, Oxford OX2 0PH, UK
44-02 23rd St, Suite 219, Long Island City, NY 11101, USA
E-mail: info@ospreypublishing.com

Transferred to digital print on demand 2010

First published 1998
2nd impression 2005

Printed and bound by PrintOnDemand-Worldwide.com, Peterborough, UK

A CIP catalogue record for this book is available from the British Library

ISBN: 978 1 85532 742 9

Military Editor: Sharon van der Merwe and Nikolai Bogdanovic
Design by The Black Spot
Index by Barrie MacKay

Acknowledgements
Particular thanks go to the Vienna team: Romain and Margot Baulesch, Thomas Posenanski and Ferdi Wöber. I am grateful to the
directors and staff of the Austrian Kriegsarchiv and Nationalbibliothek, particularly Frau Mag. Berger of the Bildarchiv (BA). Alfred
Umhey has generously assisted with pictures from the Sammlung Alfred und Roland Umhey (Umhey Collection). Thanks also for
advice and pictures to Ian Castle, Colin Ablett, Peter Hofschröer and Hans-Karl Weiss, together with John Cook, who also produced
the diagrams. Thanks to Dave Ryan of Caliver Books/Partizan Press, John Henderson, David Ruck and Dr. David Nicolle.

Editor's Note
This book contains many quotes and paraphrasing from various printed sources which for reasons of space cannot all be
individually attributed. Most of these texts are listed at the back of the book.

Publisher's Note
It is recommended that readers study this volume in conjunction with some of the following Osprey publications:
MAA 176: *Austrian Army of the Napoleonic Wars (1): Infantry*
MAA 276: *Austrian Army 1740-1780 (2): Infantry*
MAA 299: *Austrian Auxiliary Troops 1792-1816*
MAA 314: *Armies of the Ottoman Empire 1775-1820*
Campaign 2 : *Austerlitz 1805*
Campaign 25: *Leipzig 1813*
Campaign 33: *Aspern & Wagram 1809*
Campaign 56: *Eggmühl 1809*
Warrior 20: *British Redcoat (1) 1793-1815*
Warrior 22: *Imperial Guardsman 1799-1815*

Artist's Note
Readers may care to note that the original paintings from which the colour plates in this book were prepared are available for
private sale. All reproduction copyright whatsoever is retained by the Publisher. All enquiries should be addressed to:
Jeffrey Burn, Old Buittle Tower, nr. Castle Douglas, Kircudbrightshire, Scotland DG7 1PA

The publishers regret that they can enter into no correspondence upon this matter.

FOR A CATALOGUE OF ALL BOOKS PUBLISHED BY OSPREY
MILITARY AND AVIATION PLEASE CONTACT:

Osprey Direct, c/o Random House Distribution Center,
400 Hahn Road, Westminster, MD 21157
Email: uscustomerservice@ospreypublishing.com

Osprey Direct, The Book Service Ltd, Distribution Centre,
Colchester Road, Frating Green, Colchester, Essex, CO7 7DW
E-mail: customerservice@ospreypublishing.com

www.ospreypublishing.com

AUSTRIAN GRENADIERS & INFANTRY 1788-1816

Aside from the Peninsula and Napoleon's 1807 campaign, Austrian troops played some part in every major campaign of the Revolutionary/Napoleonic Wars. Despite suffering defeats against Napoleon prior to May 1809, Austrian troops, under commanders such as Archduke Charles and Paul Kray, inflicted defeats on French armies throughout the period.

Janus-like, Austria looked in two directions, also facing south against the Ottoman Turks, whose border had stabilised along the Save and Danube rivers. Although the Turkish threat had largely evaporated, just before the Revolutionary Wars, Austrian troops had been engaged in a three-year war against them. The Turks relied on mounted, mobile forces, requiring a different military approach from that used against European armies; Austrian troops had to prepare for both.

Unable to mobilise its population fully for both political and economic reasons, Austria recruited from territories as diverse as modern Belgium, the Czech Republic, central Romania and northern Italy, alongside volunteers from southern Germany and a sprinkling of Irish. The simple soldier could find himself fighting anywhere within the area bounded by Belgrade, Kiev, Brussels and Milan in terrain as diverse as the Po Valley and the Swiss mountains. Fighting could vary from the formal linear actions fought in Belgium to the desperate hand-to-hand struggles in burning villages at Aspern and Wagram.

Austria's best veterans formed the famous Grenadier battalions created from divisions attached to each infantry regiment. German and Hungarian Grenadier officers in the 1798 uniform and short Zopf (pigtail). (Mollo)

CHRONOLOGY 1788-1816

1788 Allied with Russia in the war against the Turks; victories at Semlin, Cetin.

1789 Belgrade captured.

1790 Death of Joseph II; accession of Leopold II.

1791 Peace with Turkey.

1792 Accession of Francis II; War of the First Coalition; defeat at Jemappes.

1793 Victories at Aldenhoven, Neerwinden.

1794 Defeats at Tourcoing (with allies) and Fleurus; Belgium abandoned.

1795 Third Partition of Poland.

1796 Victories at Wetzlar, Amberg, Würzburg, First Caldiero; defeats at Lodi, Castiglione, Arcole.

1797	Defeat at Rivoli; Treaty of Campo Formio; Lombardy lost, Venetia gained.
1798	Unterberger Reform Commission introduces new uniform and equipment.
1799	War of the Second Coalition; victories at Ostrach, Stockach, First Zurich, Novi, The Trebbia; defeat at Second Zurich (with Russian allies from Novi onwards).
1800	Defeats at Marengo, Hohenlinden; Treaty of Luneville.
1801-4	Archduke Charles' first reforms.
1804	Creation of Austrian Empire.
1805	Mack reforms drill and organisation. War of the Third Coalition: victory at Second Caldiero; defeats at Ulm, Austerlitz. Peace of Pressburg: Venetia and Tyrol lost, Salzburg gained.
1806-8	Archduke Charles' second reform period.
1806	End of Holy Roman Empire; Abrichtungs (drill) Reglement issued.
1807	Exercier (manoeuvre) Reglement; Dienst (service) Reglement.
1808	Landwehr battalions formed; Reserve battalions planned.
1809	War with France: victories at Raszyn, Neumarkt, Sacile and Aspern; defeats at Teugn-Hausen, Eggmühl, Wagram, Raab. Peace of Schönbrunn: loss of Illyria, Salzburg, Western Galicia.
1812	Auxiliary Korps joins Grande Armee in Russia; victory at Gorodetchna.
1813	Wars of Liberation; Landwehr form 4th and 5th battalions; victories (with allies) at Kulm, Leipzig; defeat at Dresden.
1814	Victories at Bar sur Aube, Arcis sur Aube, Valeggio; the defeat on the Mincio.
1815	Victory at Tolentino (Naples); Peace of Paris; northern Italy gained, Illyria and Tyrol recovered.

1799 infantry and a Grenadier, still in a bearskin lacking a peak. The 1798 uniform was modern in its cut. Light infantry (in background) were supposed to perform the light role, leaving the infantry formed up in line. (Seele)

THE RAW MATERIAL

The army's core was its German infantry, Upper Austrians being considered 'brave, laborious, industrious, intelligent and agreeable'. Conscription had operated across the Hereditary and Bohemian (western) lands from 1781, based on population rolls of each regiment's district. All able-bodied men aged between 17 and 40 (with those aged 18-26 taken first) were liable unless exempted. Those exempted included: nobles and priests; most skilled workers, including miners and workers in licensed factories; many townsfolk; and all free peasants and their eldest sons. The burden thus fell on junior sons of peasants and the urban proletariat.

Most regiments were garrisoned in their recruitment district, but when based outside, an officer and a group of Commandierter did the work. Until 1807 each district was divided into 16 Werbebezirke (company sub-districts); later the whole district was a single unit. Each had its own 'Military Population Book' (houses had numbers painted on the door and there was a fine of 9 Gulden if the number was not visible). The book was maintained by a Werbebezirkoffizier (officer in charge of recruitment in the district) alongside the civil authorities. Every year, between 1 March and 31 May, the Werbebezirkoffizier undertook a tour of inspection of the district, checking the list from the civil authorities of the 'individuals next selected for military service'. Anyone visited was technically 'conscripted' as they were confirmed on the military list.

Recruitment continued through the year, only ceasing when numbers were filled. Those selected were called forward, and replacements were found for incapable or absent recruits. Various ruses were attempted to avoid conscription: brought before the Leutnant commanding a recruiting party, one claimed to be the only son of an aged widow accompanied by another claiming to be his brother! Grabbed by a Korporal they were promptly thrown into the transport wagon. The authorities preferred not to take married men in peacetime, but would in war.

Those not required were 'merely visited and measured' and were left on indefinite furlough. The civil authorities could substitute those on furlough with 'tobacco smugglers, poachers, criminals intending to escape and vagabonds'. No potential recruit could go into an exempt area or abroad without express permission, on pain of a fine of 150 or 300 Gulden respectively.

Although the minimum height requirement was 165cm and medical exemption was limited, the authorities were not fussy: The 1784 Field Surgeons Regulations noted: 'if we only wanted to take those... who are robust and strongly built with a broad chest... then the number we could accept would fall very low.' Many of the best men, especially the literate, were taken by the cavalry and the artillery.

Service was for 25 years (effectively life), except for bakers and equipment suppliers, who enlisted for three years. Prior to 1802, aside

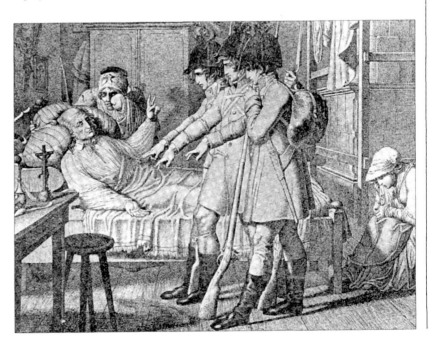

The shortage of manpower in 1813 required lifting exemptions and calling up underage men, particularly from the peasant population. (Karl Russ)

Hungarian piper recruiting. Other inducements included 'ringing handbells... persuasive patter by the officer... seductive music and a beaker kept full of sparkling wine.' (BA)

from complete incapacity, release was only possible when, through inheritance, purchase or marriage, a man acquired property or a business which he was required to run; but release was conditional on the district providing a substitute.

From 1782 to 1808 German regiments had Aushilfsbezirke (supplementary districts) in Galicia, two regiments per Bezirk. By 1802 Galicia's 'idle, stupid and drunken' population was contributing about 54,000 Poles and Ruthenes (Russians) to the army, and 11 regiments were transferred to Galicia in 1808 when the recruitment districts were changed (see MAA 176). Moravian regiments retained their districts, which supplied half of their 3rd battalions.

Hungary's (comprising Croatia, Hungary and Transylvania) army contingent rose steadily from 35,000 to 63,000, requiring 6,034 recruits per year. Renowned for their fighting spirit, the eastern provinces retained a feudal system to raise infantry, mainly from a peasant population 'as rude and savage as the animals they dwelt amongst'. In the south the 'frank and hospitable' Serbs and Croats provided 'doughty fighters [who] consumed vast quantities of strong liquors'. Officered by local Saxons, who were 'tall and more commonly fair than brown' with 'a high forehead, large blue eyes and an open cheerful countenance', the Transylvanian regiments contained a mix of them, known for their 'industry and sobriety' and Vlach (Romanians) who were 'rather lively, but of cunning, revengeful, indolent [and] brutal character... short in body, but of a strong, muscular strain [which] bears hardship with fortitude... His features are strong and expressive, his hair dark and bushy.' The addition of 'well-made brave, robust, and indefatigable' Szeckels, with their reputation for 'preceding the army and lying in ambush', made them regular advance- and rearguard troops.

Each district supplied a fixed quota, either selected by local lords from their serfs or taken as volunteers. Most were volunteers (21,000 out of 26,000 in 1790-94) rather than allotted peasants. Various subterfuges were deployed (see Plate D) to procure the numbers; foreign (non-local) volunteers received 5 Gulden. 'Abstellung ex officio' – collecting unwanted males, rogues and vagrants, anyone without papers, and renegades from Catholicism (there was no judicial sentence to service) – was widely used, and the results were delivered to the local barracks. Landowners disrupted the recruiters by describing labourers as skilled men or concealing them, but escaping serfdom in one-room clay huts produced many volunteers.

In 1781, 23,680 troops were on furlough, with 280,344 men available for conscription. Unlimited marriage, movement of peasants to towns and the Turkish wars reduced numbers to 15,963 and 69,020 respectively a decade later. By 1801 only 1 in 130 Hungarian men was serving; in the conscription lands the number of exempted classes grew, so that only 83,199 (1 in 70) were available for conscription – 20,000 short of the numbers required. Despite rounding up landless labourers and unemployed, numbers were only maintained by increased voluntary recruitment, especially in Germany, despite the ceiling on foreigners making up more than a third of any unit.

All regiments recruited volunteers (Regimentswerbung), but Italian, Walloon, and Tyrol units (mostly lost by 1797), relied wholly on it. Recruiting officers were accompanied by clerks, musicians and troops chosen from 'the most senior, the best and the finest-looking men of the regiment'. Country fairs were good sources: recruiters waited for the peasants to run out of money and get into fights, and then they would join up to escape justice. Voluntary enlistment was for six to eight years; foreigners signed up for a 'Capitulation' of six years. The bounty for western volunteers was 35 Gulden (10-15 Gulden for underheight youths who joined the Garrison battalions).

Until 1806 Austria recruited in Holy Roman Empire (Reich) states without forces. Four regiments recruited directly, but other volunteers were allocated as required. Southern Germans were regarded as particularly good troops, and because of their higher educational standards produced about half of the German units' NCOs. 'Reichswerbung' was unlimited: the station commander was sent the funds for the numbers required. Immediately on enlistment, the authorities tried to persuade recruits to stay on – an additional 12 to 32 Gulden bounty was paid, depending on how early the recruit signed up for the extra period. Enlisting for a few years and the bounties induced many Imperial subjects to volunteer at the Reich recruitment stations.

A Bavarian, von Grueber, went to the Regensburg station in 1800 to avoid a legal career: 'I saw an old Korporal of IR17 with a ring of keys in his hand. He looked at me kindly and asked what I wanted. I explained to him my determination to become a soldier.' Having asked what motivated him, the Korporal took Grueber to the recruitment officer, advising: 'As a soldier, you must always be humble, obedient to your superiors, to the Korporal as much as to the Oberst (Colonel), always treat them with respect... treat prisoners fairly, always treat foreign peasants humanely... The Korporal led me to the first floor, where the Commandant was. He questioned me extensively... Then I went on to the next room to be examined by a military doctor... he declared me fit and returned me to the Commandant, [who] ordered the Korporal to accompany me to the enlistment room... at the end of a long corridor, the Korporal opened a door and I could see in a vast space more than 20 young men sprawling on the straw, shouting, singing and yelling. On the table, some small loaves, pots of beer and bottles of brandy – 'So now, drink, eat, amuse yourself well!' the Korporal said, chuckling, as he turned round and locked the double lock of the door... Contact with these dregs of humanity made me greatly regret my decision to become a soldier... recruits are obtained partly by the lure of money and partly by the bottle... three-quarters were common drunkards, indulging in all the coarser gestures and songs. Some of them lying and snoring under the table... some saw in the jugs and bottles a great help to screeching and swearing their way to unconsciousness. This went on all through the night... as I sat unhappily on a bench in the corner of this foul room. As I didn't feel able to accept their insufferable invitations to drink and fraternise, they heaped unpleasant abuse on me and sang contemptuous songs, spilling their drinks... As dawn broke, this vulgar crowd fell asleep and I was able to have a nap on my bed. All was quiet until just before 6 am, when as the drummer beat Reveille, the Korporal entered. We were lined up in the courtyard; a large detachment of infantry... formed up in front of us and were ordered to load their weapons; their officer informed us, that if, during the march, any of us tried to escape or didn't keep quiet, they would be shot without further process. Then the group

Tambour (drummer) 1798 uniform. There were 23 drum commands. Drummers were often weak boys, but the 1807 regulations required adult males, who could hold position and beat the orders under fire. (BA)

7

marched off.' After 1806 recruitment stations continued on the Empire's northern borders.

'Lifelong service,' wrote Archduke Charles, 'produces an army which is already over-age at the outbreak of war, consisting of decrepit soldiers, who will either have to be invalided out after a few months or who are disaffected and ready to desert.' As Mandelham saw: 'most conscripts look on their future with anger and on those freed by capitulation with bitterness.' The revelation in 1802 that from the conscription provinces 27,000 men were 'absent, unwissend wo' (missing, whereabouts unknown) led to lifelong service being abolished. It was replaced by a 'Capitulation' of 10 years. Although soldiers could return to former occupations while still fit, anxiety about trained men returning to civilian life meant the reform wasn't fully implemented until 1808. In 1811 the Capitulation was extended to 14 years.

Territorial losses made some units multinational: IR44 Belgiojoso was originally recruited from its district in Lombardy. After release from Mantua in 1797, many Italians, including the Inhaber, deserted to the Cisalpine Republic and were replaced by a contingent of German Reich-struppen. In 1799, 300 Croats from the Gyulai Freikorps joined, and its recruitment area moved to the German enclaves (Vorlände). Encouraged by the French, more Italians deserted in 1801, although Italians from the Tuscan army and, along with French, from the disbanded Light Infantry battalions, enlisted joined by former Dalmatian Freikorps (including Turks and Montenegrins) plus another contingent of Reich recruits. The loss of well-educated Italian NCOs required the drafting of many NCOs from other German regiments. To maintain cohesion, German became the language of all instruction, and officers had to learn it. The departure of Polish-speaking officers and NCOs to the Duchy of Warsaw caused further problems, when IR44 became Galician in 1808 and received a contingent of 1,700 troops.

Nevertheless, most units looked homogenous. In 1797 Goethe thought: 'There were three battalions of IR12 Manfredini here, amongst which, as can be discerned from many signs, there were very many new recruits [Moravians and Galicians]. The men are almost all of the same size, a small but tough and well-built type. The regularity of height is remarkable, but even more so is their facial similarity... They mostly have narrow slit eyes which... are set back, but not deeply, narrow foreheads, short noses... the mouth wide with flat lips... they are tightly and well clothed, a lime green bush of all types of fresh foliage on the Kaskett gives a good appearance, especially when they are formed up. They perform their weapons drill... quickly and well, and it is only in deploying and marching that it is possible to discern the new recruits... Austrian uniforms comprise merely what is necessary and useful.'

IN GARRISON

Apart from Galician regiments, the infantry were usually garrisoned in their home district. Some barracks, such as IR4's Alserkaserne in Vienna, accommodated one battalion, but lack of purpose-built facilities meant most units were garrisoned in fortresses. Officers enjoyed the best local houses, with some companies quartered in houses in the locality. In 1808

German infantryman in 1809, wearing a 1769 jacket cut down to the 1798 pattern. The army had four sizes: small, medium, large and extra large – most were ill-fitting. (BA)

Working in the garrison, most troops wore simple round forage caps made from old uniforms. German infantry wore stockings below their breeches (Ottenfeld)

IR4's staff and six companies were in Wiener Neustadt, the 13th and 14th at Laxenburg, the 6th in Brunn and the rest in the Vienna suburbs, with 300 men on construction work at Buda (soldiers were regularly employed building roads and canals). 'In Hungary the troops are quartered on the inhabitants, who are obliged to find the provisions and necessities for the troops, for which they are paid according to an antiquated scale, which is far below the actual cost.' The garrison provided firewood.

The recruit was formally enlisted at the garrison, and having sworn allegiance to the Emperor, received 3 Gulden, from which he had to purchase hairbands, comb, knife and fork, shoebrushes and cleaning equipment. His pay had to cover his daily food, laundry and cleaning costs. A soldier was required to 'wash himself and certainly his hands with soap daily, and comb his hair' and 'change his shirt at least twice a week... cut his finger- and toenails diligently'.

His tunic was undyed 'perlgrau' wool (1769 Regulations), with a camisol (waistcoat) worn underneath. The regulations continued: 'The uniform [must be] cleaned daily with a brush, and each piece cleaned with pipeclay and chalk [to render it white] and dusted down, shoes were to be polished every day', and the leather maintained by 'rubbing in unsalted fat regularly'. Both uniform and weapon were to be maintained in good order and the man 'must not lose, exchange or sell any of it'. (1807 Regulations).

Those garrisoned in houses were fortunate: in barracks the man's bed was 'a wooden bed for two with a bed-end and a raised head board... on it a square pallias and straw bolster, a linen sheet, which the man could pull off to improve his uniform by cleaning it. In winter, a coarse blanket... which is like a board; in summer, he has nothing beyond his coat to cover himself with.' (Zach)

The 1807 Dienst (Service) Reglement prescribed a cleanliness regime:

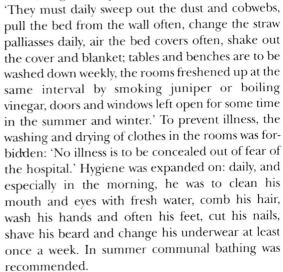

'They must daily sweep out the dust and cobwebs, pull the bed from the wall often, change the straw palliasses daily, air the bed covers often, shake out the cover and blanket; tables and benches are to be washed down weekly, the rooms freshened up at the same interval by smoking juniper or boiling vinegar, doors and windows left open for some time in the summer and winter.' To prevent illness, the washing and drying of clothes in the rooms was forbidden: 'No illness is to be concealed out of fear of the hospital.' Hygiene was expanded on: daily, and especially in the morning, he was to clean his mouth and eyes with fresh water, comb his hair, wash his hands and often his feet, cut his nails, shave his beard and change his underwear at least once a week. In summer communal bathing was recommended.

To maintain trust and discipline, the soldier was forbidden to borrow or lend anything. The men clubbed together in small messes, so embezzlement of communal funds was severely punished. To avoid temptation, 'At no time, even off duty, should a soldier allow himself to be

1790s infantry relaxing on picket duty. Often Kasketts had a non-regulation peak attached to the rear as a forage cap.

found drunk… playing cards for money or in the company of immoral women and depraved companions.' (1807 Regulations) A veteran of IR50 saw it differently: 'The general belief prevailed that the welfare of the troops depended purely and simply on endless training… cleaning, inspections, and drill from early morning until late at night, filling the drill rounds with clay or sand, polishing shoes, tying the Zopf [pigtail], beating clothes, flattening creases and cleaning were the eternal watchwords… Every Sunday and Festival there were large church parades in full kit and equipment, which from first cock crow meant ten times as much inspection in open and closed ranks, parade drill, measuring the Zopf and calling the muster by the Gefreiter, Korporal, Feldwebel and officer… In order to instil into the man the necessary attention to this pedantry, he was never allowed out of the barracks except under orders, if he had not done four to five years of this misery without punishment, which was however absolutely impossible, because the slightest failing in drill, Zopf or uniform was punished with the Hazel Stick or, when leniently, 24 hours in the guardhouse.'

In the field or garrison, no-one was allowed out without reporting it to the Fähnrich. To hinder desertion, only trusted ranks were allowed out of camp, although exact measures depended on the troops involved. In Vienna the 'Edelknaben' of IR4 enjoyed such a reputation for late-night carousing, that locals referred to black rings under the eyes as 'Deutschmeister'.

Population differences in recruitment areas meant that the establishment could vary between 2,000 and 3,000. The 1775 Regulations limited soldiers' wives to 15 per company (the Oberst had to base his permissions to marry upon that figure) who helped in the hospital, cleaning and washing clothes for their owners. They were not to accompany their husbands into the field, but this rule was not observed.

Pay and bread portions 1792

	PEACETIME			WARTIME		
	Monthly rates (Gulden/Kreutzer)					
	Germany	Hungary	Bread	Pay	Feldbeitrag (Daily)	Bread
(Officers received bread in peacetime in the Netherlands only)						
Hauptmann	71 42 ½	65 53 ¼	2	German rate		3
Oberlt	26 48 ¾	25 9 ½	2½	German rate	52	2
Unterlt	22 37	21 9 ½	2	German rate	43	2
	Daily rates (Kreutzer) and bread rations					
Feldwebel	15	10 ½	1	German rate	1	1
Korporal	10	7	1	German rate	1	1
Gefreiter	7 ½	5 ½	1	German rate	½	1
Grenadier	6	4 ½	1	German rate	1	1
Gemeiner	5	4	1	German rate	1	1

1807 rates were unchanged, except that the Feldwebels received 2 kr more and Gefreiters received 1 kr Feldbeitrag.

Pay was to be given in advance for between 5 and 15 days, although it was usually in arrears. An additional 'Feldbeitrag' was payable when hostilities began. The Empire's financial problems meant that pay, particularly of junior officers, was increasingly made in the depreciating Bankozettel notes, which were so worthless by 1809 that a pay chest captured by the French at Landshut was ignored by looters.

Austrian Measures

1 Gulden/Florin = 60 Kreutzer	**1 Wiener Löth** = 17.5g
1 Wiener pfund = 0.56kg	**1 Seidel** = 1 pint
1 Wiener Fuss/Schuh = 12 Zoll = 31cm	**1 Zoll** = 2.63cm
1 Schritt (pace) = 2 Wiener Füsse	**1 Klafter** = 6 Füsse = 2.5 Schritte (paces)

(The Schritt was measured between the heel of the forward foot and the toe of the rear shoe. The Klafte/Schritte (paces) is the distance moved over the ground.)

TRAINING

Unable to invoke nationalism, the July 1801 Officers' Instructions encouraged officers to create an *esprit de corps*. The 1807 Dienst Reglement appealed to a sense of honour, love of God and the Monarch, with the primary role of defending the Fatherland. These were impressed into the men: 'The soldier's duties, contained in the Service Regulations, together with the Articles of War, will be regularly read out in front of the men and explained to them in their mother tongue.' In this multi-lingual army, all drill was conducted with German commands. Common commands were given by drum or by signals from the flank men.

In order to instil a respect for rank, the first drill after the standing position was saluting an officer, both individually and by groups, turning the head smartly to face him. All superiors were to be addressed as: 'Herr' and then rank. Although in garrison the troops usually wore Holzmütze (forage caps), all drill was conducted wearing a cartridge box slung from the left shoulder, and Grenadiers had to wear bearskins. Learning to keep his body balanced, the recruit was taught the basic turns and then put into a small group. Drill was then conducted by numbers, running through the process slowly at first and then increasingly quickly as his proficiency improved, taking each process in groups of moves. Having mastered the basics, the recruit was taught to march. The troops marched at a formalised ordinär pace (see Plate H), using stärker for deploying. 'Marsch! Marsch!' sent the troops to dublir, required for assaults and advancing while volleying, but for no more than 400 paces. An oblique step was used to gain ground, when moving forward and sideways. Finally came individual weapons drill (see Plate E).

Continuous drill, along with improvements in weaponry and ammunition, enabled capable troops to fire three rounds a minute, and with the 1784 pattern musket up to six. Drill was hard, even for cadet officers. One remembered 'The many and hours-long drill session with a weapon weighing 12-14 Pfund, which I could not control because of physical weakness and with which I was so tormented that I rarely left the drill square without my hands covered in blood, which my instructor called "removing the inadequate flesh".'

The last stage of Abrichtung (basic drill) formed troops into ranks and Zugs with a frontage of 0.75 Schritt per man: the tallest stood in the front rank, the shortest in the second, each man's elbows touching the next man. Within each battalion the height fell away from the flanks to the centre, although each Zug's flank files comprised the ablest troops irrespective of height. The distance between the ranks was one pace, opened to four for weapons drill.

Volley fire and Exercier (manoeuvre) drill were conducted in three ranks, in units from Zug up to regiment. With the firing line halted, the rear two ranks closed up as far as possible, to reduce the blast for the first rank. At 'Fert!', the front rank man put his right foot back and knelt down in line with his left foot, bringing his weapon down to the ground in line with the left thigh. The second line moved the right foot sideways hard on to the next man's foot to make room for the front man's foot. The third rank moved as necessary to get their left shoulder in line with the second rank man's right. At 'An!', the front rank leaned back slightly. The second rank aimed close alongside the heads of the front rank, moving the right foot slightly back; the third rank aimed close up to the second line muskets and moved the right foot back, so that its toe was in line with the left heel. After firing, the first row stood up and all the ranks loaded together, the two rear ranks moving back left. Firing early was severely punished, there being 'no excuse when the next man starts to fire, because the unit's steadiness must not be lost'.

When the unit was advancing or retreating using the normal or oblique step, fire was by half-company or smaller. On the command 'Peleton' or 'Halb-companie', a sub-unit moved with large paces forward from the line at dublir, followed by 'Halt!' and the firing drill. The others moved at the shorter and slower 'Chargierschritt', so if advancing, when the volley was fired, the main line would have caught up and the next unit moved forward.

As well as rank fire the troops could maintain a continuous rolling fire by file (Lauffeuer). By the time the last file of the fourth Zug of a company had fired, the first Zug had loaded and was ready to fire again. There were separate drills for fire in squares by Zug and in narrow defiles. Firing by Zug to the left flank, while marching obliquely or by file, required pulling the trigger with the left finger while the right hand supported the musket.

The infantry retained a firm belief in cold steel. Ordered to dublir, the Sturmstreich (attack drumbeat) was beaten or the command 'Fällt das Bajonett!' shouted and bayonets lowered at about 50 paces from the enemy. The weapon was snatched quickly from the shoulder to the horizontal position with the right hand, and thrown into the open left hand with elbows close into the sides and the lock moved up under the shoulder. Keeping their muskets at Hahn in Arm, the reserve line would follow the main lines at 150-200 paces, halting as the others went to dublir. Once in melees, the musket butt and sabre were deployed.

The 1769 Regulations stated: 'The common soldier is a machine and must remain so.' At the extreme, 'In one regiment served a Korporal,

1798 Hungarian infantry with muskets shouldered 1769-style, so that the stock neck could be grasped with the right arm horizontal. With a fearsome reputation, Hungary's troops were never available in sufficient numbers and there were high levels of desertion during the Second Coalition War. The trousers hook together at the bottom outer seam. Note the three tent pegs on the right side of the backpack.

who was known throughout the army as Korporal Teufel [Devil]... the most cunning torturer of soldiers who has ever worn an Austrian uniform... If there was a parade, he would form his men up an hour earlier than the others and there was no end to the inspections, drill, carping and reprimands, during which hefty blows, shoves and Lunghiebe (chest blows with the cane) were struck, as a Korporal could do this as he pleased; they were certainly not in the regulations, but aside from a few, his superiors were happy to turn a blind eye... If the regiment was on guard duty, then the soldiers initially waited impatiently for their detachment and those whom Fate placed under Korporal Teufel were close to despair, for 24 hours of hell and many blows awaited them for the slightest misdemeanour.' (Ellrich) Although unwise in this case, the man could complain to his immediate Korporal, and the complaint could progress through the ranks to the Hauptmann. Knowing of the problems with supplies, complaints about shortages of bread, pay or uniforms 'must not be made, but the soldier must be content knowing that the problem will be resolved in time and his pay made up... because a soldier is obliged to experience good and bad times for the state'. (1807 Dienst Reglement)

The 1806-7 Regulations humanised discipline: 'All forms of mal-treatment and heavy-handedness in the drilling of a soldier are firmly forbidden. Brutality is usually evidence of some lack of knowledge and destroys that self-respect which must be at the very heart of a soldier.' Accepting that men could vary, if any fell behind, they were to receive additional drill and instruction once the others had completed.

The major drill changes came in new regulations in May 1805 (refined into the 1806 Abrichtungs Reglement). The musket was carried with the arm extended and the ordinär speed was increased. The gait became 'natural, unrestricted and unforced', making marching 'the normal ambulation [which] will not tire any soldier, as soon as he equates marching merely with walking'. The dublir was to be used for all changes of formation and assaults. However, lack of training forced many troops to change formation at the intermediate Geschwindshritt.

From 1806-7 superfluous ceremonial and drill, including firing while advancing at the oblique step, was abolished. The front rank remained standing, and the second moved both feet to the right to fire so that each man's left shoulder was behind the right shoulder of the front rank man. The ranks remained at 1 pace distance, as musket barrels were long enough to avoid damaging the front rank, but were opened out to 2.5 Schuh for all training. The ablest men formed the third rank, which didn't fire. As the drums beat, they took their weapons to 'Hahn in Arm', so that the lock rested in the crook of the left elbow after loading. The minimum fire from larger units was by half-company, not Zug. The widest frontage for evolutions remained the division, but enlarging or

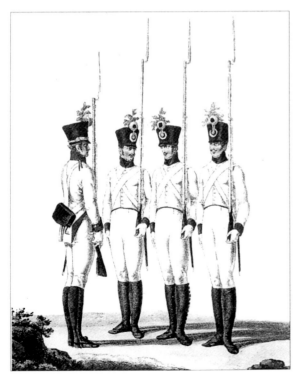

Holding his musket with his right arm, a German NCO instructs soldiers in 1808 uniforms and 1811 shakos (the right-hand soldier wears the original 1806 pattern). Muskets were held with arms fully extended being moved up as here in the first movement c.1815. (Umhey Collection)

Large-scale manoeuvres were conducted in training camps, such as Traiskirchen near Vienna. (BA) Right: A column led by its band marches at half-company intervals. As on campaign, tents are erected in two blocks. As weapons could not be taken inside, each company had four gun tents, comprising a truncated cone shape 2m high and almost 2m in diameter, the top of which was closed off by a wooden, tinplated disc; each tent held 40-50 weapons. Kobell's painting of a camp in 1805 is shown in Campaign 33, p.14.

reducing frontage was now done in one change, instead of by stages. When advancing and retiring, volleys were by companies. Lauffeuer continued to be conducted in three ranks, the rear rank aiming high.

From 1806 accurate shooting was emphasised. The musket was held so that the soldier could see down the barrel to the sight. Each man only received 10 live rounds per year, although designated Schützen (Sharpshooters) – two Korporals and 12 Gemeine per company – fired 25.

In 1790 losses in the Turkish wars had reduced many battalions to below 200 men, which forced units to draw off officers and NCOs to train new recruits in the third battalions. Insufficient time to drill the troops and a shortage of NCO cadres for reserves and reinforcements remained a constant problem. By 1797 recruits were being despatched virtually untrained. Four Hungarian battalions consisted 'of peasants loaded on to wagons... none can handle a musket... three-quarters of the men, unused to a soldier's life and in part not clothed properly and not equipped with mess-tins, arrive in the hospitals; the rest throw their muskets away out of fear and ignorance when they see the enemy.' (Archduke Charles)

Although most training was conducted in the garrisons (boy soldiers joined the Erziehungshaus), after the 1792-97 war, drill camps were revived in various terrain around Vienna (1797 and 1801), Turas (1801), Laxenburg and Moravia (1802) and Minkendorf (1804). Many improvements emerged from these camps, especially skirmishing, and field exercises at Aviano (Italy) in 1805, where line troops played the role of Grenzers.

'The 1802 camps clearly demonstrated the high proficiency of the common soldier', although Archduke Charles recommended 'more proficiency in loading... Marches on the centre were not best executed, the heads emerging too slowly from the front and the following Zugs are too concerned about being behind them, instead of marching forward and closing up behind one another gradually, the wings therefore having to sway outwards.'

Paces (paces per minute/metres per minute)		
	1769	1806
Ordinär	60/44.5	90-95/67-70
Stärker/Geschwind	75/56	105/78
Dublir	120/89	120/89

Field days could turn violent: at Minkendorf 36,000 men assembled: 'The army had divided into two parts, operating facing each other. [The cavalry] intended to charge a battalion of Grenadiers formed in square in front of the churchyard. Having broken in good time, these troops were to rally behind a wall and, by their fierce musketry, repel the Kurassier. But the programme wasn't passed to the Grenadiers: instead of dispersing at an appropriate moment, they remained formed up in square and fired on us... As many of them had loaded stones in their guns, men and horses were wounded on our side... Seeing their own men fall, the cavalry couldn't be restrained and charged in hard. The battalion was hacked into and the Grenadiers replied to the sabre blows. When they rallied behind the cemetery wall, it was only after much blood had flowed on both sides.'

Training was impeded by the financial need to send large numbers of troops on Urlaub (furlough). During the 1790s only 60% of internal troops were serving during peacetime; the other 40% were on Urlaub after basic training. Urlaubers received no pay; NCOs were only paid if on Urlaub for a maximum of two months – one month's pay on departure, one month's pay on return.

Turnover was not high – about 200 per year in peacetime – the majority ending their terms. In the earlier years the 3rd Battalion, including those not fit for field service (Hungarian 640-strong 4th Battalion until 1798), trained recruits and provided replacements for wartime casualties. Their more capable soldiers brought the first two battalions up to full strength and the 3rd Battalion took in all the 1,400

Financial restrictions meant there were no training camps from 1805 until after the wars. Gun tents have been erected between the tents. (Castle)

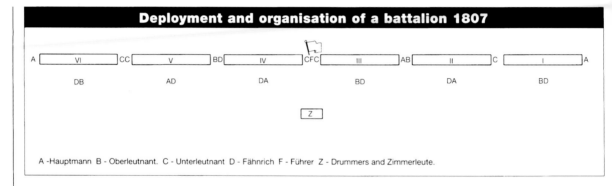

Deployment and organisation of a battalion 1807

| A | VI | CC | V | BD | IV | CFC | III | AB | II | C | I | A |

DB   AD   DA   BD   DA   BD

Z

A -Hauptmann B - Oberleutnant. C - Unterleutnant D - Fähnrich F - Führer Z - Drummers and Zimmerleute.

Under the 1807 changes, the companies were now arranged numerically. Other supernumerary NCOs were usually positioned between the battalions. (see also p.32)

Urlauber and new recruits (1,240 Hungarians) needed as well as creating the 17th and 18th companies and (for German units) a reserve division of three officers and 720 men. Reinforcements went to the regiment in Ergänzungstransports (groups of reinforcements).

In December 1801 regiments were reduced to 80-100 active men per company, and by August 1803 some were down to 25. At that stage new recruits were being called in, given basic training and then placed on Urlaub. This formed the basis of the Reserve system planned in 1808: Reserve battalions composed men liable to call-up or recently released, who were to be trained by the depot for four weeks in their first year and three weeks in their second.

'From these reserves will be drawn replacements for wastage, those having been longest in the reserves being called up before recent recruits; for those of equal service, joining the Line will be determined by lot... Before a man joins a regiment he will have been trained for some years already as a reservist, so that... in war, the increase in the complement will no longer be drawn from untrained troops.'

The 1809 war intervened. Urlaubers were called in from November 1808, but many failed to appear, so most 3rd Battalions were made up of new recruits with only limited training. Most were initially of no use in the field. Used for reinforcements, many had to be marched off to Moravia for additional training before Aspern. Hofkriegsrat instructions of September 1812 resurrected the Reserve plan (Hungary was excluded), creating the 1813 Landwehr battalions. During training, these recruits received Line pay and allowances but had to provide their own clothing (Galician units received smocks and forage caps, retaining the 'Reserve' name).

As the IR63 geared up for war, there was a steady inflow of partially trained men. 'Urlauber joined us daily; they were detached into four companies and drilled twice a day with weapons... [We] received 1,200 new recruits [in July 1812], who were designated as Reserves, drilled with weapons until the end of October 1812 and then beurlaubt... In Spring 1813 the Reserves were called in and drilled, so the companies [of 3rd Battalion] were up to full strength.' (Rzeib) The Oberst-Lt. added: 'In August 1813, just six weeks before marching out on campaign, [we] received 1,300 newly raised [Galician recruits]. As a result of the strenuous efforts of all the officers, we were able to train these men in this short time so that they could be used against the enemy... despite this process being made much harder because the regiment lacked the raw material for NCOs due to previous transfers to other units.

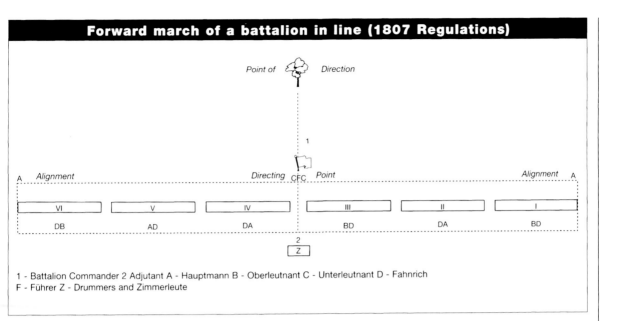

Forward march of a battalion in line (1807 Regulations)

Point of Direction

Alignment — Directing CFC Point — Alignment

| VI | V | IV | III | II | I |

DB · AD · DA · BD · DA · BD

Z

1 - Battalion Commander 2 Adjutant A - Hauptmann B - Oberleutnant C - Unterleutnant D - Fahnrich
F - Führer Z - Drummers and Zimmerleute

On the march, alignment was maintained by marching on a distant object, led by the flag 6 paces ahead with officers guiding the flanks.

FLAGS

Battalion flags showed the unit's location and provided a clear reference point for NCOs directing the line of march. In battle they were the rallying point for an unformed unit, a drill practised by scattering the unit. The drummers then beat 'Vergatterung', which was also the signal for the troops to fall in for drill.

Line battalions carried two standards, reduced to one in 1808. The presentation of new colours was a cause of great celebration in the unit with feasting and fireworks. Prior to 13 October 1807 (after which flags were returned to the depots), it was customary after the consecration of new standards that old flags belonged to the men (*Gemeine*), who kept them for 24 hours before presenting them via a Hauptmann to the Oberst, in return for some barrels of wine. Wartime presentations were hurried: losing two flags at Dresden (in August 1813), IR56 fought the winter campaign without standards. New flags arrived on 27 February 1814 as French troops were attacking. 'The flags... were immediately taken by the Oberst and Major amidst joyous shouts. As the fighting continued and enemy cannonballs knocked down rows of men, the regimental chaplain spoke the Holy Blessing over the flags, which were unfurled and flying high for the first time. Weapons in hand, the troops gathered around the flags, swore loyalty with a thousand voices, followed immediately by a general "Hurrah", which could be heard over the guns, and moved forward.' (Anonymous officer) The flag's importance led an IR3 Gefreiter to tear his battalion flag from its pole and swim the Danube at Regensburg in 1809 to avoid capture.

LEADERSHIP

A 1790 company comprised: Hauptmann, Oberleutnant, Unterleutnant, Fähnrich, Feldwebel, four Korporals, two Tambours (drummers), eight

Gefreite, a Zimmerman and 91 Gemeine; Grenadiers were to maintain full strength at 99 Gemeine (no Fähnrich nor Gefreite), taking infantry as required – in 1795 IR4's Grenadiers received 50 veterans from the 3rd Battalion.

The Feldwebel was effectively the company adjutant, responsible for internal discipline, administration and drill. He organised distribution of bread in the rear tent line or at a convenient place in the garrison. The 1807 Regulations permitted him to beat men with his cane (Hazelstock; from 1803, Spanisches Rohr) but directed that he should be 'more concerned with positively influencing the men by his example'.

Companies were divided into two half-companies and subdivided into two Zugs, each commanded by the senior Korporal – one of the most tiring jobs in the army. This wide range of responsibility included: correct drill and discipline; ensuring regulations were complied with; and checking cleanliness, uniform and kit. Every day he reported to the Feldwebel on the state of his command. As the company size and the number of Korporals increased, Zugs were broken down further into small Korporalschaften, headed by Korporals.

In wartime each company expanded to six Korporals, 12 Gefreite and 160 men (raised to 200 men late in 1792), although many companies had three officers and 120 in the ranks. All command places had to be filled, so where no supernumeraries were available, the army operated a Stellvertreter (deputy) system. In peacetime Vize (temporary) rank holders were nominated. These temporary rank holders would then bring the company to wartime strength. Officers' places could be filled by Kadetts or NCOs, although Feldwebels had to remain in place, with Gemeine filling vacated NCO posts. This created a training school for both NCOs and officers to assess whether a temporary rank holder was suitable for holding it permanently. Two Vize-Korporals were nominated from Gefreite, one Vize-Gefreiter from among the Gemeine. The Grenadiers nominated one Vize-Korporal from the Gemeine, filling additional posts with supernumeraries or able soldiers.

Wheeling to the left from line into march column at company intervals with the flag following the outer flank of the third company. (1807 Regulations)

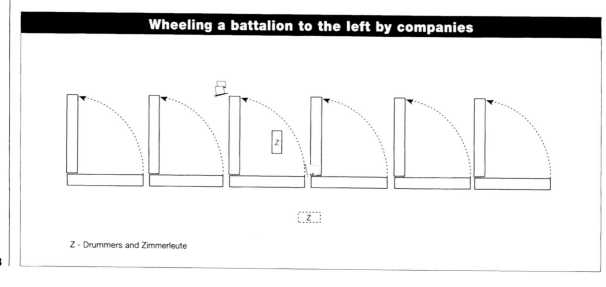

Wheeling a battalion to the left by companies

Z - Drummers and Zimmerleute

Originally a man of at least 12 years' service, freed from routine tasks, a Gefreiter supervised Kameradschafts of men and helped newer recruits, collecting the mess food money. In the field, Gefreite led the pickets and patrols. Having the primary role of setting an example to the men under them and keeping discipline, the post became the first stepping-stone to promotion for able Gemeine.

The 1807 organisation increased the company strength to: one Feldwebel, six Korporals, seven Vize-Korporals, two Tambours, a Zimmerman, eight Gefreite and 153 Gemeine (173 Hungarian). In wartime 20 Gemeine and two Korporals were added, the latter as supernumeraries. One peacetime Korporal became an additional Feldwebel and all seven Vize-Korporals took full rank. Another Zimmerman and four Gefreite were also appointed, and the command had to designate at least two Gemeine or Kadets to fill vacant posts in action. The Grenadiers had 13 Korporals (having an extra peacetime Vize-Korporal) but no Gefreite with 120 Grenadiers.

All NCOs had to be literate, so the increasing company size and NCO requirement promoted education within the battalions: 'As [IR63] lacked NCOs in 1813, I was allotted 30 men from the Reserves, who had some ability and could speak German. I taught them reading, writing, maths and other necessary subjects to qualify them as NCOs.' (Rzieb)

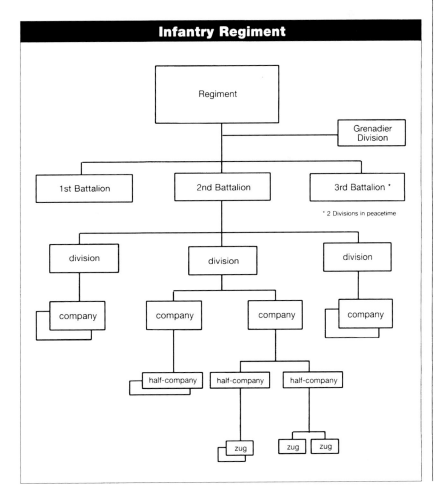

Infantry Regiment

Regimental organisation: Hungarian battalions had four battalions pre-1798. In 1805, each regiment comprised four infantry and one Grenadier battalions, reverting to the normal organisation in 1806.

Officers

Although mostly German or Hungarian, Baron Vautier noted: 'The officers [were] from many nations; among them in 1794 I found French, Belgians, Luxemburgers, Walloons, English, Irish, Poles, Croats and Swedes.' Others were Spanish and Danish. By 1798 they were regularly criticised: Zach identified a lack of military spirit and a wish not to lose:

'The Fähnrich concerns himself with food, remu-

Korporals and Gefreite led small raiding parties; larger patrols were led by junior officers. Rivers often were the best means of movement. (Seele c.1799) (Umhey Collection)

neration and rewards… Advancement is determined by intrigue, favours or comfortable routines… When the Obersts and Hauptleute gather, they speak twice as much of pay scales as of drill and rarely of war… The officers are distant from the men; they don't live amongst them, but in the town… they do not know their men, they don't know their names, they have no regard for them, they are not concerned about them and so, no respect, no trust is returned.'

Many left camp whenever possible: officers billeted in Lucerna in 1799 went 'to La Torre. There were many beautiful cultured women in the town, who happily spoke with us under their parents' gaze, and innocent games and dances made the time race by so quickly that we rarely broke up before midnight.' (Rauch)

After the Second Coalition the officers needed attention: 'The 1802 drill camps [demonstrated] the complete inability of the officer corps.' Criticised for spending more time banqueting than training, during the September 1804 camps officers continued to show 'they didn't know how to use their own abilities in independent action'. (Reports)

Officer cadets came from three main sources: Fahnen Kadetts (Fähnrich from 1798); graduates of the Wiener Neustadt Military Academy or the Ingenieurs School; and kk ordinäre and regimental 'ex propris gestellten' Kadetts. The ordinäre cadets were sons of serving officers, but ex propris included ordinary soldiers appointed by the Oberst. These cadets could become NCOs or officers depending on their ability (taking interim NCO positions). A shortage of graduates from the academies prompted Charles to found subsidiary cadet schools in 1808, taking pupils from the middle and lower classes. Once commissioned, officers received further training in the regimental Erziehungshaus (training school) in the garrison.

Although Hungary's feudal system meant a peasant was unlikely to rise above Korporal, western regiments were flexible. Both losses of officers and insufficient numbers emerging from the academies meant that ex propris cadets steadily increased, with Feldwebels being promoted for bravery. Regimental Adjutants (senior Feldwebel) were automatically promoted, when the rank became commissioned in March 1803.

The Landwehr of 1808 required the commissioning of many serving

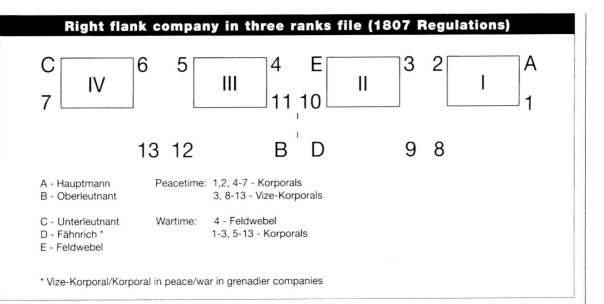

Right flank company in three ranks file (1807 Regulations)

C   IV   6   5   III   4   E   II   3   2   I   A

7   11 10   1

13 12   B D   9 8

A - Hauptmann   Peacetime: 1,2, 4-7 - Korporals
B - Oberleutnant   3, 8-13 - Vize-Korporals

C - Unterleutnant   Wartime: 4 - Feldwebel
D - Fähnrich *   1-3, 5-13 - Korporals
E - Feldwebel

* Vize-Korporal/Korporal in peace/war in grenadier companies

Right flank company in three ranks. Under the 1769 regulations, in wartime:
E – Feldwebel
A, 2, 5, 7, third rank behind 2 and 5 – Korporal
C – Kadett (flank companies) or additional Korporal (others)

NCOs. Battalion commanders could appoint officers from capable recruits; one was Rzieb, a minor official who was appointed a Fähnrich after conscription into 2nd Bunzlau Landwehr. When the Landwehr was disbanded, these former civilians were allowed to join the army, Rzieb joining IR63. Other volunteers were commissioned directly, including von Ense, appointed a Fähnrich in IR47 by its Oberst, despite lacking the linguistic knowledge – 'Most of the men spoke only [Czech].' A north German, he 'bought the equipment of an officer killed at Aspern and exchanged my hat for a shako', but felt that most officers were culturally ignorant.

More NCOs were drafted to officer Landwehr battalions of 1813, and instant promotion became possible: at Valeggio on 8 February 1814 a battalion of IR4 marching off by Zug was struck by canister. For behaving bravely and steadying the disordered Zug, Feldwebel Eisen of 15th Company was promoted to Fähnrich on the field.

Once commissioned, soldiers could gain a Patent of nobility as a Freiherr (landless noble) for long service, outstanding bravery or on reaching the rank of general. Oberleutnant Johann Georg Freiherr Fastner von Neumarkt (1769-1811) started as a boy soldier of 14. Winning the silver bravery medal as a Gefreiter at Mauberge in 1793 and gold as an adjutant at Verona in 1799, he was commissioned in 1803. As an Oberleutnant he was awarded the Cross of the Maria Theresa Order, together with his Patent of nobility at Neumarkt in 1809.

Although few commoners (including Mack, Hiller and Brady) became generals, junior officers included relatively few nobles; most Freiherrs had gained a Patent for bravery or were sons of ennobled fathers. Even in the fashionable IR4, of the 80 junior officers in 1788, two were Barons and 11 were Freiherrs; of the 134 serving in 1813, two were Grafs (counts), 17 were Barons and 15 were Freiherrs.

Combined with improved officer training – notably the Beiträge zum practischen Unterricht im Felde (Essays on Practical Field Instruction), junior officer leadership improved markedly in the later army. Archduke Charles appreciated its capabilities by 1809: 'The best possible spirit prevailed amongst the troops. They were well ordered, disciplined and more manoeuvrable than previously... But this was certainly limited in its effectiveness to the individual regiments and their commanders. Large troop formations had not been assembled nor trained in acting together.'

REWARD AND PUNISHMENT

Originally, rewards for distinguished conduct were financial, but in 1789 Joseph II instituted the Bravery Medal: Gold brought lifetime half-pay and Silver a 50% increase in service pay. Each came with a citation. That of Feldwebel Anton Losert of IR18 at Aspern read: 'The devastation wreaked by enemy artillery had already made IRs 18 and 15 waver, when this brave warrior seized the flag from the wounded standard bearer, shouted 'Mir nach' [follow me] and the salvation of these regiments was directly attributable to his heroic example.' Gemeiner Seibt of 9th Company won the Silver and 6 ducats for capturing a French eagle at Wagram. IR18's medal tally in 1794 demonstrates the army's reliance on its NCOs: one Feldwebel and one Korporal won Gold; five Feldwebels, 10 Korporals, one Führer, one Gefreiter and three Gemeine won Silver. Nothing changed over the period. At Valeggio (1814) three Feldwebels, one Korporal and one Gemeiner from IR4's 1st Battalion won medals for the storming of il Furoni.

Corporal punishment, both judicial and non-judicial, was common, although rarely administered in battle. The Korporal's Hazelstock, the symbol of authority, which was the thickness of a musket calibre (18.3mm), was the main implement wielded, as necessary, to keep the men in line. It was not permitted to beat a man over the head, in the face or over the feet. Veteran NCOs were appointed Profoss (Provost) to handle military arrest and investigation for the Auditor (legal officer) with a small team of assistants. The authorities ordered instant arrest for inciting or attempting desertion, or if an excess of money or goods suggested a man was a thief.

In 1807 military courts were reformed. A literate Gemeiner or NCO could serve as a Mitrichter (assessor) on the three-man tribunal. After the hearing, the Auditor would give an assessment of the case and Articles of War. Fighting was punished with 60 strokes; discarding a weapon with 50 strokes. Offenders were also confined to the guardhouse without pay. Serious offences earned demotion, a term in a fortress such as Munkacs, or execution.

Punishment was conducted among the company tents or, if in garrison, in front of the Hauptmann's house. The company was assembled and the beating administered by a Korporal. Gefreite were not beaten publicly, but privately in front of the NCOs. Korporals and higher ranks were not beaten, but arrested and tried after a suitable warning.

Unknown junior officer 1810. The influx of capable men into the officer ranks greatly improved leadership. (BA)

Hungarian infantry officers (Mollo, 1798). The cane remained the officer's symbol of authority until 1803. There was no official pattern of pistil until 1809.

Francesca Scanagatta: born 1776, graduated from the Neustadt Academy in place of her brother and reached Leutnant without discovery until pensioned off in 1801.

In 1807 corporal punishment was abolished, but the antics of IR2 in robbing peasants, along with a series of fires, prompted its return in June 1809. Throughout, the Articles of War provided for capital punishment for most serious offences. Under a directive dated October 1798, deserters' property was seized. A problem among Italian and Hungarian troops during the Second Coalition, desertion only attracted the death sentence in wartime. Out of the Mühldorf bivouac during the night of 13 April 1809 deserted Tambour May with Gemeine Chaque and Depree, all foreign volunteers. Caught by patrolling cavalry, the next day, in front of the assembled IR4, they were executed by firing squad.

ON CAMPAIGN

Once orders were received, companies formed up over three days. Most regiments were ready within 35 days. To gather the 40 Urlauber per company and extra equipment required two to three months. Until 1798 they had to provide one Korporal and 29 men (1/10 Grenadiers) as Handlangers supporting the gun crews.

Moving out in the 1790s, the troops marched about six hours a day. By 1800 in Italy, this had risen to 10 hours: 'At 9 am the… battalion marched off by Zugs, the division to which I belonged leading. One company kept to the right and the other to the left of the main road, always in line with each other, leaving the road clear for advancing cannon.' (Rauch)

They presented a fine sight: 'Several regiments of soldiers passed us here on the way to join the army in Italy [in 1814]; they appeared healthy and well dressed, wearing a slip of laurel or pine in their caps.' Another observer from Landshut in 1809 saw 'The streets were packed full of troops who sang Bohemian and Slavic war songs [and] over the following two days, streamed through the town.'

Marching was a shock to newer recruits: in home territory Major Mahler of 6th Battalion, IR49 found in 1805: 'During this strenuous march, I lost many men, some of whom had been left behind because of fatigue, some out of fear, as most were still newish recruits who headed off home.' Training would continue: in September 1813 'the men were drilled daily on the march and in sharpshooting on reaching camp.' Muskets were kept loaded, and were cleaned every two to four weeks or after rain.

The army was reliant on supply magazines, so prior to 1805 it was tactically limited by the need to be within five days' march of supplies. These were connected to the army by supply columns, but local purchase was also used to fill Proviant wagons and to move fresh water. Food shortages were a major factor in the rising desertion at the start of the Revolutionary Wars: '190 recruits have deserted from the infantry… and they fired on those who stood in their way. The reinforcement transports always arrive about half the strength that they set out with.' (Archduke Charles)

In 1792 each regiment had 14 Proviant wagons, a Feldschmeide (field smithy) and six four-horse ammunition wagons and 54 packhorses per company; reduced by 1809 to the Feldschmeide, ten four-horse wagons and 26 packhorses per regiment. Packhorses kept to the side of the march column, carried tents, food and the first ammunition reserves. The Proviant wagons carried provisions back and forth from

The True Comrade (IR4 memorial)
Vienna): Feldwebel Fuchsgruber
rescues Oberlt. Baron Synoth at
il Furoni in 1814, winning the
Gold Bravery medal.

1813 German Grenadiers from
IRs 3 and 36 (Klein). The 1811
Bearskins are combed
downwards and show the
common yellow pattern on the
reverse. The Feldwebel (centre)
wears his Gold Bravery medal
without a ribbon. (Nürnburg
Stadtmuseum)

the main supply column to replenish the regiment's uniforms and shoes (200 pairs of shoes, 75 pairs of gaiters, 200 trousers, 200 pairs of underpants and 800 shirts). At the rear of the column came a collection of contractors, sutlers and meat sellers, who were reluctant to get close to the front line. In Bavaria in 1809 Rosenberg found baggage wagons and cattle in the main column, camp followers who 'wandered about in the villages ahead of the troops and foraged there as they wished'; mules carrying cooking utensils, and packhorses 'wedged themselves in between the infantry Zugs'.

The army supplied bread (baked in mobile ovens), some water and meat. Each soldier drew a two-day supply of bread from the column magazines, stuffed into a calfskin backpack with spare clothing (stock, shirt, pair of stockings, and forage cap), an oil flask, personal belongings together with a ball extractor and a touchhole pin.

Bread was usually black and of poor quality. The troops preferred meat, which was sold to them from the Schlachtvieh cattle herds accompanying the army at 1 Pfund for 5 Kr. The rest, including drink, the troops had to buy from the sutlers. Food varied, from staples like dumplings and sauerkraut to specialities such as Moravian wild duck or Vienna fried chicken. The troops also foraged and bought supplies from the local peasants, at the same time gathering intelligence from them. Regulations permitted looting in enemy territory, although it was limited by political considerations, notably in Bavaria.

In the 18th century both sides would withdraw into winter quarters around early November and re-emerge around early April, but from 1796 they were exposed to winter campaigning (most wore forage caps under their headgear). Forming Merveldt's rearguard in 1805, IR4 arrived at Lunz, where the troops camped in the snow. The first hungry

Marching through Eger (Bohemia) at the start of the 1809 campaign, the infantry looked smart in their greatcoats. (BA)

Months on campaign produced a more varied appearance. A soldier buys a drink from a peasant woman, as a Korporal tries to get him back into the column. A Serb Freikorps soldier (left) has joined the unit. (Seele c.1795) (Umhey Collection)

soldiers had acquired all that the local peasants could offer, and there was nothing left for IR4. One Fähnrich even found that the offer of his gold watch could not procure a piece of bread. The road to Neuhaus had become iced over during the night – hundreds of soldiers pulled the guns up this difficult track on dragropes, as the horses were exhausted by lack of forage.

Russian allies could be worse than French opponents: 'Hardly had [the provisions] been prepared than we were roused at 3 am [to retreat]. Now our sufferings doubled. Shortages of necessities increased markedly because although they received their provisions separately, despite all our efforts to oppose them, the Russians seized the bread and forage rations from the men there of our force, and even carried off officers' baggage and wagons into their camp.' (Mahler)

The more mobile warfare from 1809 forced more requisitioning, but often the terrain did not offer much and the troops did not really know how to exploit what was available. With continued reliance on the trains, they ran short of many supplies. In 1809 the troops drew three days' bread and one day's biscuit from the magazine wagons, supported by two days' supplies on the Proviant wagons. Food was cooked some days in advance; the soup was consumed and leftover meat carried with them. Shortages were then exacerbated because the cumbersome supply trains could not keep up over

awful tracks, which continuously climbed and descended, causing frequent halts on the march.

The 1807 diet prescribed: breakfast – ⅙ measure of brandy; lunch – soup, ½ Pfund of meat, and a supply of vegetables comprising cooking flour, ¼ Pfund of rice, ⅛ measure of barley and/or local green vegetables, a half measure of beer or quarter measure of wine; evening meal – beer or wine as at lunch plus two Pfund of bread. Following a march or drill, soldiers indulged in the Austrian speciality of 'Abkochen' (cooking what was available in a small pot over a large fire) up to twice a day. Meat and vegetables were cooked together to create something similar to the Carniolean 'Black Broth', thick with vegetables. Fähnrich Höpler noticed: 'There were so many insects around that it was not unusual to fish louses out of the soup.'

Beer, most (cider) and wine were widely drunk, as were spirits: 'I have never seen the Austrians fight with such a rage; they were all drunk with brandy,' wrote Massena in 1796. On the eve of Austerlitz, Allied troops turned to the clear Slivovitz. Two weeks earlier, near Hollabrunn, French soldiers had broken into a wine cellar between opposing lines. Within a short time 'the Russian, Austrian and French soldiers could be seen suspending hostilities in order to drink from the same cup'.

Tobacco was supplied from local depots. Members of IR42 (western Bohemia) 'begin in the earliest state of youth to acquire the habit of smoking, so general in Germany'. Mandelham revealed the priority: 'One must experience it for oneself to know… what a harsh fate it was to be without bread for a few days, but endure it with patience and resignation, but be in no doubt that when they lack tobacco and eventually have the choice between buying bread and tobacco with their last coins, they would hand over the money for tobacco… I am one of those who can happily spend a day without bread, but certainly not an hour without a pipe.'

The worst problem was the clothing shortage – only half of what was paid for was supplied. As the weather worsened in 1793, Prince Coburg noted: 'Two thirds of these poor brave men are without greatcoats.' Embarking on the 1796 German campaign, the army lacked 69,127 pairs of trousers, 267,228 pairs of underpants, 337,337 shirts, 49,014 pairs of gaiters, 14,313 pairs of shoes and 30-40,000 greatcoats. At Emmingden 3,000 troops fought barefoot; many lacked trousers and gaiters. Muskets supplied in 1797 were 60% overweight.

The quality of clothing and shoes was often so bad that two articles had to be worn together. 'In many shoes, the sole is made of cardboard, so that in the first rain, the shoe separates; the jackets and shirts are full of loose threads and the trousers often so short that I myself can hardly wear them.' (Archduke Charles, who was five feet (153cm) tall) Footwear was in such short supply in 1809 that FML Jellacic had to requisition 50,000 pairs in Munich (see Campaign 56). Frequent rest days were required, both to allow supplies to catch up and to repair footwear and clean equipment.

Infantry and wounded irregular relaxing in camp in the 1790s. The right side man carries his bread in a separate bag and has a 1773 metal waterbottle. Troops drill in the background. (Kobell) (BA)

Clothing that was made properly was heavy and, combined with water shortages in mountains of Italy and Tyrol, made the summer heat of northern Italy almost unbearable. Malaria was rife there: in the swampy Balkans it killed 5,000 troops, while dysentery struck thousands more. Suffering only a handful of casualties in 1788, IR4 lost six officers and 1,000 men to disease; another 185 died over the winter.

After icy winters in northern Europe, the troops endured the hot summer in Germany but some campaigns were different: opening in 1792, Hohenlohe reported 'the unceasing extremely heavy rain, accompanied by storm force winds, [made] everything soaking wet and the road so ruined that each day 200 shoes are lying on the road'. He added: 'The soldiers must march barefoot.' After marching in snow mixed with the rain into Bavaria in 1809 and bivouacking on sodden fields, typhoid raged – III Korps' sick list ran at a constant 6.5%.

Pauses in campaigning created impromptu marketplaces, where locals could bring their wares. Before Wagram the troops could be seen 'busy, some keeping their weapons and equipment in order, others engaged in other work, but most were being drilled. From early morning onwards, small and large units were being exercised… Three times a day, the regiments formed up for prayers [by Catholic rite; IR53 had a Greek Orthodox priest for its Serbs] with weapons; repeatedly the drums summoned the Feldwebels and Korporals to attend the issuance of orders.' (Von Ense)

Off-duty, 'the soldiers had enough time to root around; they were well practised, and what one didn't know, another taught him… they used their ramrods and sabres to check everywhere over like robbers and on the slightest impact, they could not be put off digging, even if sometimes it went unrewarded.'

On campaign each regiment had 534 tents. Each was allocated two bundles of 16 Pfund of straw to last two weeks, then one bundle for the

Pre-1798 Grenadiers on the march, carrying their weapons in various positions. The device on the front of the bearskin cover was usually painted. (Ottenfeld)

next two, although new straw was obtained as required on the march. Wood and straw were bought in, but the army relied on sympathetic locals. On 3 December 1805, after Austerlitz, two Grenadier battalions (from Merveldt's force) held the outposts and skirmished with enemy cavalry. Only around 9pm, in exceptional cold and stormy weather, did the troops receive wood and some straw, and around midnight local peasants brought food for the troops.

The weather caused major problems, especially with the tents, which could became prematurely damaged. With continuous marches and the camps not erected for weeks in the unceasing rain of 1792, the tents rotted on the animals, and the troops were lumbered with a long train carrying unusable equipment. Archduke Charles surveyed the damage in September: 'You can have no idea what our troops look like. It's rained every day for a month, so that the rain penetrates the tents. Many of our men have no shoes, all the uniforms and tents are full of holes and begin to smell.'

If the enemy were not close, the troops would scatter into cantonments. Mack decreed tents for only half the men in 1805, and four years later Archduke Charles forbade the erection of tented encampments in Germany. The troops had to bivouac or seek quarters: 'Officers were sent on ahead to allocate the billets and bivouac sites on the Vils river... To get the troops under cover as quickly as possible, a cantonment had to be worked out promptly with the aid of men familiar with the area... the Korps had to be accommodated within a [one-and-a-half mile] radius of Aich (the forming up point). In this encampment, each regiment had about 10 houses at its disposal, and it appeared to

Having interrupted French soldiers in a tavern, Austrian troops and a Hussar relax with their pipes and a couple of trophies (Seele). (BA)

During a break on the march in 1805, infantry relax, enjoy a pipe and obtain water. Note the Grenzers on the left in two uniform styles. (Umhey Collection)

have very little in the way of life's requirements.' After little restful sleep on the soaked sites, the marches continued.

Buildings were sparse at Eggmühl – 'The Austrian camp consisted of straw huts, which they had hastily constructed from straw gathered into the local villages after the previous harvest; many bivouacked under open skies around the fires.' In the wait before Wagram, more solid structures were built: 'Troops lay under the open skies; in the middle of the regiment, just one tent was erected, which served both as a field church and for the Oberst. All the remaining officers and men had to make do with mud huts, which had something of a roof of turfs and leafy branches. One occupant, von Ense, described the conditions: 'I slept the first night in an earth hut with my Hauptmann and another officer.' The huts were 'very poorly built; they had removed a quite a lot of ground around them… there was hardly enough room for three to four men inside'.

Russia in 1812 (see Plate I) became the graveyard for 7,000 men from Austria's Auxiliary Korps (all Line regiments were Hungarian or Galician); 'The villages offered the army little or almost no resources; rarely could a man find drinkable water; man and beast were day and night tormented by gnats and midges. The Russians had cleared all supplies from this area; the heat of July was followed by cold rain, so that the troops suffered from frostbite in the middle of summer and had many sick… the only succour for hunger were abandoned and partly burned enemy carts, as they contained biscuit, brandy and other supplies… the wounded could not be transported; they sank into, disappeared and suffered a miserable death in the mud.' (Weiden)

Schwarzenberg tried to establish a purchasing system to supply: one and ¾ Pfund of bread, ½ Pfund of meat and ½ Pfund of meal or one Seidel of either oats, barley, peas, lentils or beans. On days when vegetables were cooked, they were followed by ½ Pfund of bread and a double meat ration, a quarter Seidel of brandy, ¹⁄₄₀ Seidel of salt, ¹⁄₂ Pfund of tobacco and ⅛ Seidel of vinegar. Supplies were to be drawn to last between one and four days, with Proviant wagons carrying two days' meat and four days' rations of bread or biscuit as iron rations, to be consumed at half-ration. In reserve, when foraging failed, there were 20 days' supplies in medium-sized carts, but as Weiden observed: 'The small oxen and bad roads meant that these wagon columns… fell steadily further behind, scattered or even, once the load was consumed, the peasants drove off with the oxen and en route had committed many misdemeanours. A large part of the food perished and the troops used hardly any of it.' Bread was soon in short supply, some troops going without for days, so by mid-August it was substituted with vegetables or meat. 'Even officers used to the frugalest nourishment went without the heavy bread, and to maintain their strength sometimes drank some wine.' (Weiden)

Desperate shortages led to cruel excesses against the population, but fierce justice followed – the penalty for robbing and plundering (including robbing the wagon trains) was 100 strokes and, later, death.

Tents were made of linen thread, being about 2m high, 1.9m wide and long, enough to accommodate 4-5 men. Each officer had his own tent made of semi-bleached twill fabric with floral-patterned lined canvas, whose size and fittings depended on rank. When not in use, each tent was kept in a canvas tentbag, which was packed together with the cooking equipment for transport on the packhorses. (Posenanski)

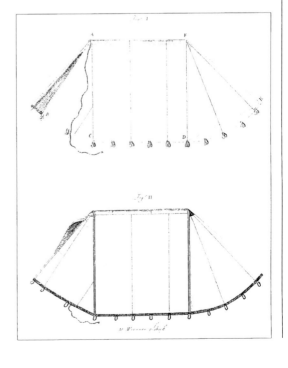

By 31 October, 12,000 men were inactive; half its effectives by the end of November. Schwarzenberg reported: 'Only the energy and example of the officers has up to now prevented even greater problems.' The lesson was learnt. Entering Switzerland in December 1813, all troops were to be supplied with eight days' bread and two days' vegetables. Traders supplied all other requirements on a designated scale.

TACTICS

In the last war against the Ottoman Empire, each battalion had its artillery, 78 Spanische Reiter and 15 Jägers. Fighting the mobile Turkish army meant the Austrian infantry could form square quickly and often closed up the columns to solid Masses (which were unlikely to suffer from inadequate Turkish artillery). Positions were held in squares of up to 10 battalions, but usually single battalions. Attacks were mounted in close order at a slow pace, employing steady fire. 'As soon as the Turks are heard approaching, the troops move against them, irrespective of any superior numbers, for this mob only induces confusion.' (1787 Field Instructions)

The formal warfare of the 18th century was based on manoeuvre and on maintaining the alignment of long lines with correct intervals. The troops marched in columns on the widest front possible, fighting battles deployed in two Treffen (lines) of regiments, usually with a third reserve force. Linear tactics emphasised attack in line – usually parallel to the enemy – although each side tried to advance obliquely against the other. Endeavouring to outflank the opposition, the 1769 Exercitum Reglement provided for the first Treffen to be extended with battalions from the second, moving forward in Masses (closed columns).

Fighting in long lines made command and control difficult and reduced army manoeuvrability. The main control problem was caused by smoke, as the troops could not see signals nor what their colleagues were doing. The first volleys were controlled, but gradually fire became less cohesive. To maintain effectiveness, volley fire was limited to 300

1790s Grenadiers, technical troops and infantry in forage caps in camp, most still wearing their sabres and bayonets. (Castle)

paces. The artillery, moving up to 100 paces ahead of the line to permit a wider angle of fire, handled more distant targets. Once the infantry opened up, guns were manhandled back to their line positions, firing after each volley as the men reloaded. When infantry were in a defensive position about 100m behind the guns, they would only start firing if the artillery came within enemy musketry; then the infantry would advance, firing on the flank of the gun line. If the line was moving forward, the guns went forward to lay down fire for the battalion to take the ground.

The attack was conducted by volley and advance, with the troops carrying their weapons at the shoulder, or Hahn in Arm, while marching. The number of infantry projectiles fired at less than 100 paces was increased with Flintenkartasche – three small balls fired together against both infantry and cavalry. Defence against cavalry was in three-rank-deep squares (or an oblong with divisions at front and rear, and one company each side). If cavalry approached within 10 paces, the first two ranks were to level their bayonets, while the third rank continued to fire.

Skirmishing was mainly the preserve of light troops, although a few companies of line troops were allowed into skirmish order for attacking villages and in difficult terrain. They were supported by formed units and had to re-form when ordered. Few skirmishers were used in the Turkish wars because of their cavalry. If individual Turkish skirmishers appeared, then sharpshooters were placed among the Reiter to pick them off.

The Revolutionary French enjoyed advantages in number and guns. In response to their skirmishers, Coburg's 1793 Instructions despatched small groups from the third rank. Believing three lines to be unnecessary against poorly trained opponents, in 1794 Mack recommended using the third rank to form multipurpose reserves which could be used to reinforce points threatened by heavy columns, for plugging gaps, flank protection and skirmishing. Near Tournai on 11 May 1794 in the early hours, the fire of small arms and cannon started and lasted until 2.30 pm. 'From [IR7], the third line was dissolved into skirmishers, which established continuous fire against the enemy.' The main battle on 22 May was 'largely fought by small arms; with the exception of the Grenadiers, almost all the infantry were utilised as skirmishers, whose fire lasted 15 hours'.

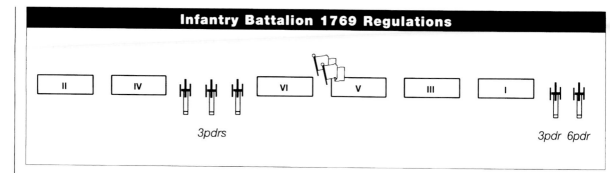

3pdrs   *3pdr 6pdr*

Mack also maintained that the Austrians' superior discipline would allow an attack in fog or at night with unloaded muskets, to throw the French into confusion. After overrunning French outposts near Mannheim on 18 October 1795, the Austrians mounted a night attack in fog 'such that no man could see more than a few paces ahead and could only work out enemy positions from shouts and fire from their posts'. Advancing silently, the muskets were not loaded until the men faced significant resistance; then, because of the fog, 'firing occurred in all directions and so, some shot fell into the column moving alongside'. Led by four Grenzer companies, the main column was attacked by Davout, but the Austrians had extra support: 'Thus we advanced, led by the able Hauptmann Neumann, as the senior in command, who always marched at the head of his troops, setting an excellent example, right past the French left, who were firing fiercely into us, without firing a shot, then moving over the causeway with bayonets pointing at the enemy, we cleared the place.'

By 1796 the long lines were being broken down into brigades, but closed up formations formed the basic tactic, reflected in Archduke Charles' Observationspunkte: 'Regular drilled and solid infantry, if they advance in lengthened paces courageously under artillery protection, cannot be hindered by scattered skirmishers. They must charge neither with skirmishers nor Zug fire against the enemy line, except when the latter can be most effective, and with the greatest speed while maintaining good order, attack the enemy hard and overthrow them.' In 1800 Zach decreed: 'Only a few skirmishers are necessary to the front, but behind them closed-up troops.' However, on 17 July drumbeats were introduced to control them.

The greatest changes arose from the Italian campaigns, where bad roads, waterlogged meadows, ditches and trees made control of the

1769 infantry battalion with small artillery pieces between divisions. The companies were arranged for manoeuvres and changes of formation based on the right flank. Each company was formed up three ranks deep.

From the 1790s, troops were drawn off the third rank in large Zugs (platoons) for a variety of purposes. Under the 1769 regulations, the entire third rank turn to one flank and extend the line, half a rank moving behind the other. When in two ranks, the front rank did not kneel to fire. Two ranks were used to defend earthworks where there was insufficient room.

Forming Zugs from the third rank of a battalion (1807 Regulations)

Z

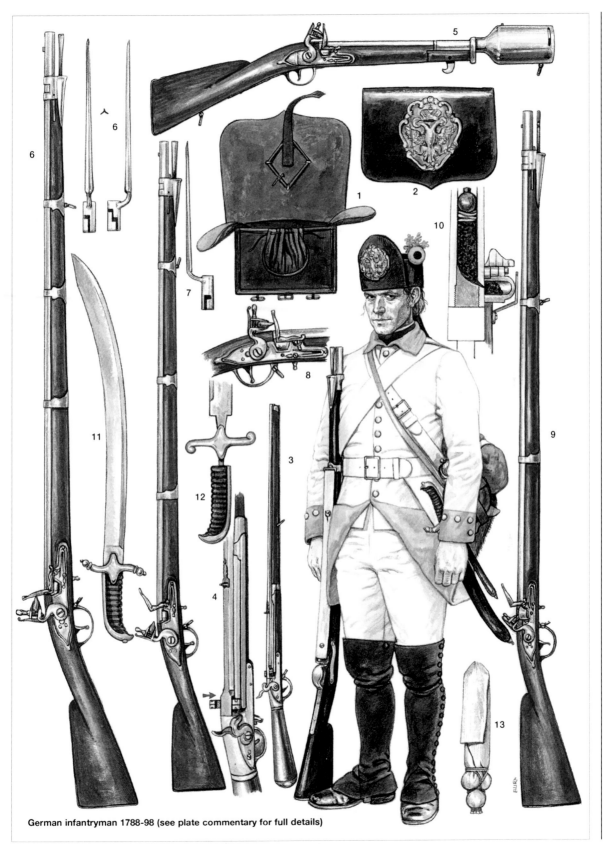

German infantryman 1788-98 (see plate commentary for full details)

A

1788-91 The Turkish Wars

B

Hungarian infantryman 1798-1810 (see plate commentary for details)

C

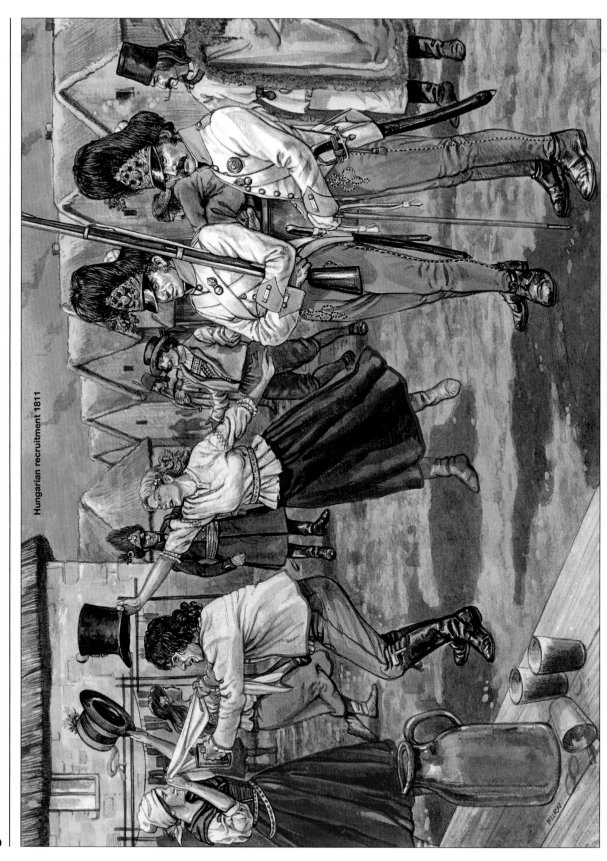

Hungarian recruitment 1811

D

Recruits firing muskets (see plate commentary for full details)

E

Austrian troops at Aspern village 1809

F

Hungarian Grenadier and Zimmerman (pioneer) 1798-1816

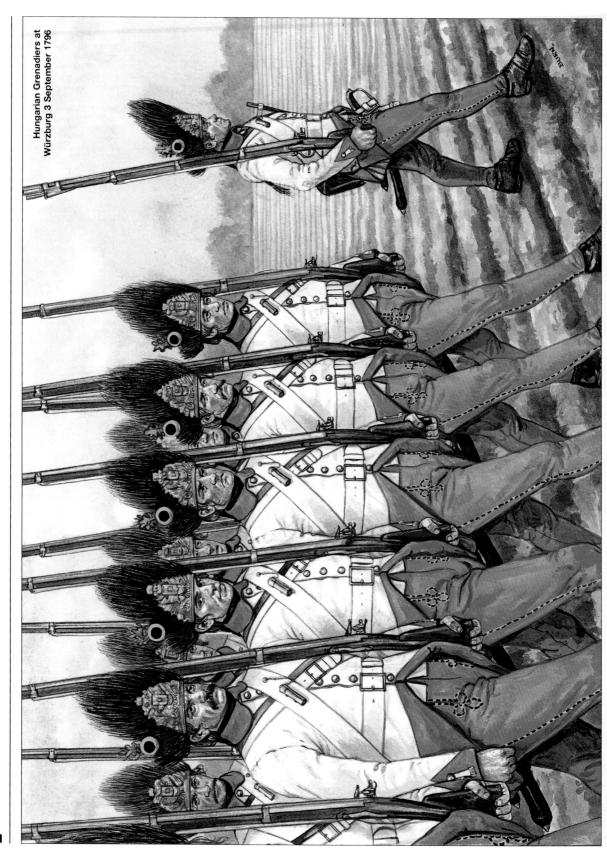

Hungarian Grenadiers at
Würzburg 3 September 1796

H

Harsh conditions on the move in Russia 1812

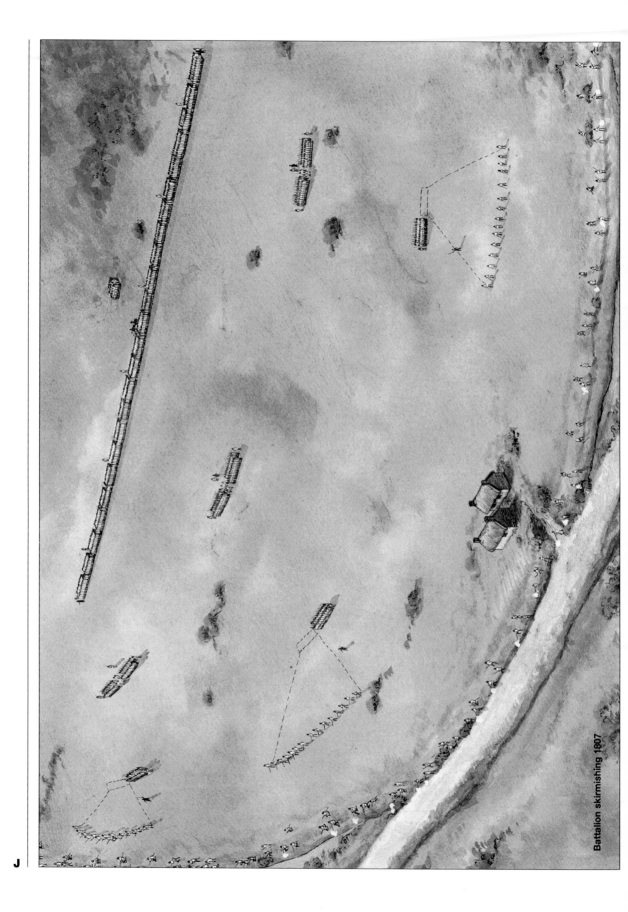

J

Battalion skirmishing 1807

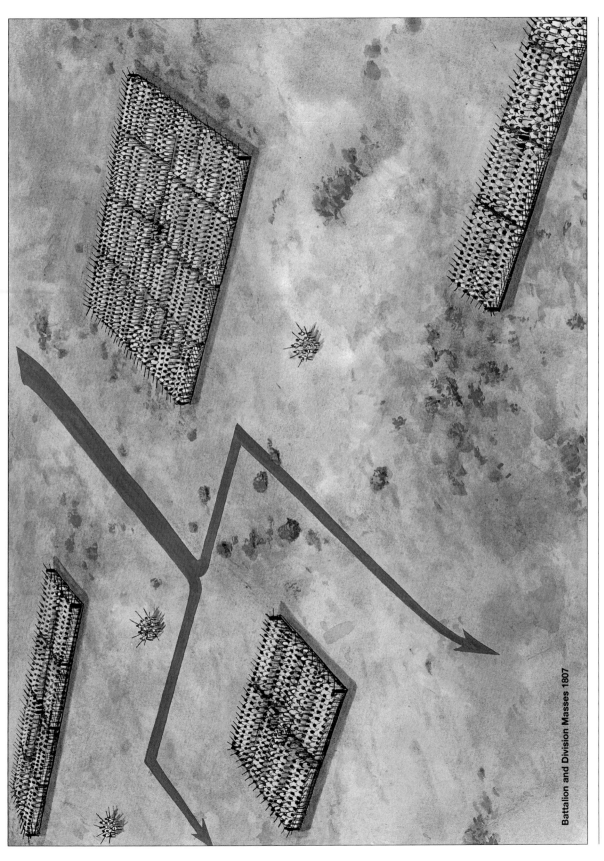

Battalion and Division Masses 1807

K

L

Grenadiers and infantry in camp c. 1811

1790s Hungarian infantry skirmishing, although one should always be fully loaded. Note the Zelthacke axe in the backpack. (Ottenfeld)

troops more difficult, so formations became more compact. Although the 1807 Regulations emphasised that, 'The line is the proper formation for infantry permitting the best use of its weapons' there was increased use of Masses as battlefield formations. Having lost cavalry superiority, the 1807 Exercier Reglement reintroduced Division Masses – two companies in six-deep formations – instead of squares. A revival of Prince Eugene's tactics against Turkish cavalry, they were the means to form a compact defence quickly from line in battle.

However, the ever larger formations and numbers of troops increased battlefield use of columns. Approaching the enemy, march columns closed up to half-company intervals and then fully (with two paces separating each company), creating a 'Battalion Mass' as action became imminent. Closed-up columns had always been used for moving columns in restricted terrain, but the 1807 Reglement emphasised their use to facilitate any advance by making control easier, to defend against cavalry and to concentrate large numbers of troops in restricted terrain or against a specific point. Formed at Aspern, Masses made short advances against cavalry and shattered the charge of six Cuirassier regiments (see Plate K).

Battalion Masses were vulnerable to artillery, and after Aspern Archduke Charles ordered: 'In the plain, the order of battle of the infantry is… Masses by companies; in the direction of the enemy a small screen of skirmishers can be deployed. Should a Mass suffer too many casualties from artillery fire, then I leave it to the brigade commander to

Officially, under the 1807 regulations, Masses enabled troops in line to form an anti-cavalry formation quickly with Zimmerleute and musicians in the centre. However, it rapidly became the main battlefield formation.

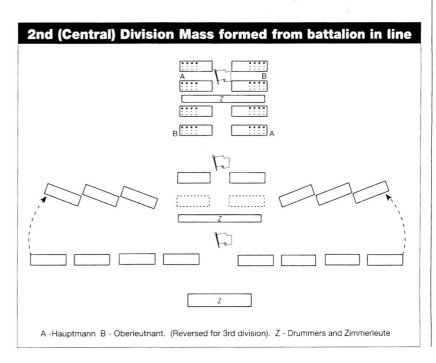

2nd (Central) Division Mass formed from battalion in line

A -Hauptmann B - Oberleutnant. (Reversed for 3rd division). Z - Drummers and Zimmerleute

Reaching the main enemy firing line beyond the forest at Stockach (25 March 1799), Grenadiers refuse to let Archduke Charles lead them further. Charles had instituted their use as concentrated reserve divisions to be committed to key points in 1796.

reduce the depth or, if not threatened by cavalry, to deploy into line.' Where a large frontage had to be held or the Masses were likely to be hit by artillery, Battalion Masses were divided directly into Division Masses, and this became the preferred formation.

In 1812 tactical philosophy still directed that the troops should advance and close with the enemy in column. 'The change from column to line should not happen before the moment when the latter can get into range.' Schwarzenberg's Instructions of August 1813 brought a clear shift from lines to Masses as offensive formations. The second Treffen and all reserves had to remain in these formations throughout.

Despite skirmishing training from 1807 (see Plate J), after Schneidart, in 1809, Rosenberg believed the Austrian troops 'are not fully prepared and too incapable of helping themselves. They are too used to being in closed lines and to acting automatically on the word of command, but they must be capable of relying on their own initiative.' In 1812 Schwarzenberg maintained: 'To dissolve battalions into skirmish order would... be a mistake. In open ground, 20-30 skirmishers will be enough to hold enemy skirmishers from the front of the battalion or Mass. In restricted ground, they can be increased to [one third] of the battalion, but the other [two thirds] must remain closed up in one or more reserves depending on the terrain... If the enemy is repelled, they are to be pursued with a third or at most [half], and the other half must form up quickly and only follow up slowly and in good order.'

Nevertheless, the troops were becoming more flexible: '2nd Battalion IR14 (at Hanau on 29 October 1813) were moved forward to support the Bavarian skirmishers in front of the Lamberwald. 'When the Bavarians were driven back, the skirmishers of this battalion moved forward, established a lively fire and halted the enemy advance... The retreat was conducted steadily and in good order and was followed by the whole regiment over the Kitzing bridge, 2nd Battalion positioned in Masses there, because the enemy cavalry were trying to force the bridge with artillery support.' 2nd Battalion pulled back down the Frankfurt road and 'formed up in three masses to cover the cavalry and a 12pdr battery.... the enemy cavalry risked an attack on the battery... however, a murderous volley from the 2nd Battalion forced them off... [On 31 October, attacking Hanau], Oberleutnants Scharff and Batte, with 80 volunteers, formed the advance-guard with the Jäger... The rest of the regiment marched up to the Rathaus... but [one and a half] companies moved on to the Frankfurt gate and took the bridge by storm at the point of the bayonet.' (From IR14's Oberst's Report)

The Grenadier battalions, formed into divisions in 1796, were the army reserve. Although many of them were drawn from the capable men who formed the third rank, the 1807 Regulations specifically forbade

ABOVE **German infantryman on outpost duty at night. Copied from a Seele picture of c.1795, Kuntz was more impressed by the Hungarian trousers and boots he has wrongly added. Most men were clean-shaven.**

BELOW **Outpost duty had its compensations, especially for this Korporal commanding a detachment in southern Germany. (Seele) (BA)**

them to fight as skirmishers, since 'they represent the main strike force or could determinedly defend a threatened point', to be committed only when required. 'Muskets at Hahn in Arm,' said one soldier at Aspern, 'these old battle-hardened soldiers advanced without firing a shot' against French batteries on 22 May. Frequently they formed rearguards on difficult retreats. Four battalions put up fierce resistance as Massena tried to force the Durnstein pass near Einod in 1797. They stood for several hours 'unmoved under a hail of cannonballs and canister, although they lost many men', long enough to allow the main body to negotiate the valley.

OUTPOSTS AND PATROLS

Alongside light troops, line infantry performed outpost duty – 200-1,000 paces out (1,500 paces in the direction of the enemy), with pickets as far out as 4,000 paces, and supported by cavalry. 'The numerous camp guards occupied thin outpost lines out front and only as darkness fell was the quiet broken by their different shouts [about every 15 minutes], "Wer dar? Patrull vorbei".' (Von Ense)

Sleeping or drunkenness on duty were severely punished, and until relieved, sentries were not to eat, drink or smoke. Only during bad weather were the posts permitted to pull back under some protective cover. 'When firing or a major incident occurs and the picket is not able to inform the main post, they should aim high and, where necessary, fire three times.' (1807 Regulations) At night the sentry would challenge: 'Halt! Wer da?' He would then raise his musket into the firing position and prepare to pull the trigger. The average misfire rate was 15-20%, prompting the contradictory advice that if they saw enemy cavalry, sentries should then blow smoke from their pipe in the air. Thinking the powder in the pan had ignited, the rider would ride confidently at the infantryman, who could then fire at very close range.

The army used a mixed advance-guard system for the early contacts with the enemy, with reconnaissance groups (Streifpatroll) comprising one battalion and/or two squadrons searching ahead and raiding.

Outpost clashes pointed to bigger actions. On 13 June 1800, 'from dawn to dusk, the thunder of small and large cannon could be heard constantly about an hour's march away. This was coming from a major outpost clash at Marengo, and was the clearest sign of the approaching battle of the next day, for which we were ordered to be ready.' (Rauch)

INTO BATTLE

As engagement drew closer, 'The withdrawal of our outposts [at Aspern 1809] confirmed that the enemy were attacking: both battlelines moved forward against the French with bands playing. The generals galloped along their units with the spirited cry "Children, now is the time, forward courageously". It was not long before the black-blue columns of French could be seen everywhere, like ants rising out of the ground.'

Enemy artillery would have the first effect: on 22 May a Hauptmann in IR15 observed: 'The enemy had only his batteries advance in an immense black line against us, intending to smash our infantry with heavy artillery fire.' At Wagram an IR4 officer felt its full effect: 'At 8am on 5 July the enemy heavy batteries opened up and we received some truly serious hits... artillery fire is grievous, because in the designated position, nothing can be done against it. Our own guns had insufficient range.'

Outposts and patrols were often a combination of line, light and mounted troops. Hungarian infantry and Jäger zu Pferd enjoying a drink c.1800 (Kobell) (BA)

Closer to the frontline, a Fähnrich of IR49 was more concerned about the French troops: 'Around 3am the French debouched at all points and sent their skirmishers towards us... We watched the French army deploy as if by magic before our eyes. Maintaining a steady distance, as the French deployed, we fell back en echequier in Battalion Masses and our brigade occupied the plateau... of Markgrafneusiedl.'

The troops could face a march before engaging. Rauch recalled at Marengo: 'The action had already begun as the roar of cannon had been underway for over an hour and enemy balls were hitting us at the entrance to the bridge. When the regiment had only advanced a short distance, we moved into cultivated fields, broken up by ditches, wheat and bushes, the view was very restricted in all directions... Ignoring the obstacles, we attacked ferociously and the musketry was so intense, like I have never heard before. Within a few hours in which they held their designated position against all enemy attacks, the regiment lost 25 dead and wounded officers plus 700-800 men. I came through uninjured but my coat and clothes had holes from several musket balls... We saw part of our cavalry fall on the enemy rear and a group of at least 1,000 prisoners passed by as our regiment began its advance and you can imagine how much this sight raised our morale... The regiment marched along the road through Marengo village; both sides were littered with cannon with shot-up wheels, corpses and piles of horse cadavers. The happiness and joy of the officers and men had spread right through on the news of victory... As the force deployed outside the village, the artillery was moving forward, flattening fields and vines, through which we often had to cut our way with sabres, against the increasingly wavering enemy, into whose lines the artillery fired fiercely. The sight of the victoriously advancing troops was wonderful; they looked like they were moving on the parade ground and the march continued uninterrupted across this lovely plain for some hours.'

Fortunes changed suddenly: 'The enemy attacked us with a frightful shout. Aside from the terror and gruesome scenes of murder, I had a feeling of pride... for as the enemy attacked, overturning our whole deployed line and forcing everyone to retreat, my company still stood for a few minutes amidst a whole mass of French, who fell on our isolated position, but I and my Oberleutnant still ordered fire by half-company, then I closed my men up... and began to retreat as though on the drill square.'

For the new recruit 'the first action is of the greatest importance: It is a moment when he gets to know himself... all his senses are very busy, so overwhelmed that he is in a daze, not properly taking in the whizzing, whistle and sound of the balls, not noticing the men falling either side of him.' (Ellrich) Even mounted officers saw little: Major Mahler (IR49) found himself at Austerlitz at around 7am 'in such thick fog that one could hardly see [fifty] paces ahead. A lively exchange of fire could be heard, but it was impossible to distinguish which part of our Allied army had attacked or been attacked by the enemy. [Later] we could only vaguely see that the Russian columns were formed up in lines in front of us and that the French, who were uniformed similarly to the Russians, were advancing against them… Hauptmann Till was despatched… to see what the French were doing in the fog and saw the Russians were retreating in disorder.'

As the French struck the Austrian line, 'to drive off the assault, I had my battalion, which was formed up in closed column, move forward on to the hills and as we were threatened from in front and the flank, I advanced to protect the flank. As the enemy skirmishers realised this advance was happening… their fire evaporated. Hardly had we deployed into line than I noticed that the enemy were preparing a frontal attack. As they began their advance shortly afterwards, I ordered some volleys to be fired and halted their advance… Then, with the nearby battalion of IR55, I counter-attacked. In advancing we came under heavy fire… which killed many. Because of these losses and as my exposed left flank was under heavy attack by the enemy, my battalion began to buckle, but I managed to reinvigorate the men and keep them closed up and prevent them from falling back… As a result of some volleys from us, the enemy fire reduced, making the movement of wounded to the rear less dangerous. In the midst of my battalion, an enemy musket ball suddenly felled my Führer… Schömdler saw a French officer [attempt] to carry off the flag from the Führer lying on the ground. He attacked him with his sword and struck his hand so that he let the flag fall.' (IR55 retreated.) 'I found myself entirely alone and had my remaining troops form closed column' (to withdraw).

A second Treffen regiment's initial role was supporting the first. In the centre of I Korps' second line, as the French attacked at Wagram on 5 July,

RIGHT **Worth a battalion in French sources: Joubert was felled by a 12-man patrol from IR4 Deutschmeister under Korporal Strakate at Novi (August 1799) (Castle)**

disordering the first line, IR42's commander 'formed the two battalions into Division Masses at this vital moment but he was wounded. Major Fromm took command [and] had the "Sturmschritt" drumm-ed, and drove the enemy back over the Russbach, sup-ported by the troops from the first line, who were rapidly rallying.' (Anony-mous officer)

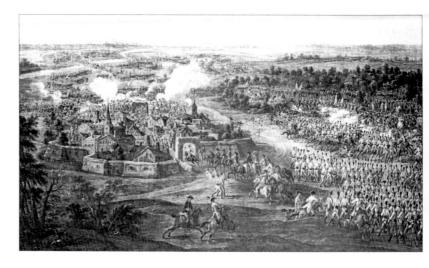

Other tactics were used against French artillery. 'The infantry were ordered to lie down and the enemy cannonballs initially hit little. But as the enemy marched steadily forward, the regiment got into action.' (Ense)

Many battles, like Wagram, lasted more than a day. 'Small arms fire continued through the twilight until it was completely dark and at that stage the artillery fire ceased... [IR42] remained in bivouacs on the north side of the Russbach on a battlefield which was covered with the corpses of men and horses – wounded and dead – friend and foe inter-mingled with the debris of army equipment and weaponry of all types.' For others: 'In the night of 5-6 July we stood along the Russbach... and lay in the grass on roadsides with weapons in hand. The night was beautiful, the men slept and the bivouac fires slowly extinguished, both ours and the French.' (Anonymous Fähnrich of IR49)

Dawn broke early and found IR42 already on the move, but the fighting only began between 5am and 6am: 'The regiment was posi-tioned close behind the village of Aderklaa (in the first Treffen) and remained formed up in Masses until midday under dreadful cannonfire. Around noon, the enemy stormed Aderklaa and were surprised to see the Masses positioned so close behind as they spilled out of the village.

The French halted and fired a salvo of ball at the Masses, which because of the short range, mostly went high over, wounding or killing all the officers' horses behind and Major Fromm himself. Soon after the first salvo, the "Sturm-schritt" was being beaten amongst the Masses. They advanced with fixed bayonets and the village was recaptured, only being evacuated on the general retreat.' (Anonymous Fähnrich of IR49)

Over at Markgraf-neusiedl, the IR49 Fähnrich 'received a sheet of paper, which had been passed from regiment to regiment, on which had been written in pencil, "We are victorious. The enemy is retreating. The days of Aspern and Essling are being repeated. I expect my left wing to show itself worthy of my confidence. Charles." Our brigade commander, GM Mayer… read this out in a loud voice and fired up the troops, who

1799: As Austrian infantry and Grenadiers secure the forest north of Stockach, cavalry charge across open ground to the east, backed by infantry and artillery. Infantry marched in column, adopting the widest practical frontage. (BA)

were keen to get into action, still more with a short speech. He reminded us of the laurels won at Schwarze Lackenau… From our plateau, we could see over the whole battlefield and so could clearly see the large columns that were wheeling right out of the enemy centre and heading for our wing… The murderous struggle began. We threw back four assaults, but each time the attack was renewed with fresh and larger numbers of troops. Our standards passed from one hand to another; each of us had already taken hold of them and carried them forward in new attacks; our brave Oberstleutnant, who had already lost two horses shot from under him, was fatally wounded with the flag in his hand and only with the greatest exertion could we hold on to the plateau… We already had 30 dead and wounded officers; our ranks were terribly depleted. From the enemy side, more fresh columns advanced; we were on our own, because all the available troops were in action to strengthen the right wing… also increasingly large masses of [enemy] cavalry were

IR49 deployed in both divisions and half-battalions evicting French troops off Schwarze Lackenau (May 1809). (Baulesch)

turned towards [us]… Suddenly the enemy brought a previously masked battery into action against our flank and we came under canister fire… The regiment was reduced to a weak third of full strength, but we retained our flags… Whoever remained on the battlefield, who wasn't dead, was wounded. In order to retreat, we had to force our way through the burning Markgrafneusiedl. In amongst the flames, chased by enemy guns, we could only keep our men together with great effort and in this way, continuing to fight, we fell back.'

The 1809 battles marked the end of cavalry's real effectiveness: at Aspern Oberst König of IR33 saw enemy cavalry advancing towards 1st Battalion. 'I concluded a short and succinct speech with the instruction that no-one was to fire without my command... As the enemy cavalry approached to within 50 paces, I ordered "Front rank, lower bayonets. Second rank, take aim, fire". As the enemy stopped short and halted, then I ordered "Cease fire!", which everyone did as though on the drill square... I then ordered that no-one should leave the ranks to loot [fallen officers].'

'The example of IRs 39 Duka and 14 Klebek at Neumarkt (April 1809), which attacked two French Chasseur à Cheval regiments at the point of the bayonet shows what a determined infantry confident in their capabilities can do.' (BA)

'Lacking the time to form Mass, the [IR2] battalion awaited the [cavalry] attack with great composure with lowered bayonets. The enemy advanced to within 30 paces, where they began to waver and they were thrown into disorder by a well aimed volley, fell back but then rallied after a short distance. As a further charge was expected, disregarding the canister fire, we formed Mass and the position was held.'

The troops' confidence in small unit tactics had grown by 5 July 1809: 'One of [Charles'] adjutants shouted "Volunteers forward". Immediately, almost all of Hauptmann von Marais' company were prepared to go. We thought it would be effective to attack the enemy battery, which was approaching through the cornfield in front of us, and cheering with loud shouts, we raced down the slope... we were to guard the crossing over the Russbach, but not to open fire yet as the enemy was not yet that close... Dissolved into skirmishers, behind willow tree trunks and high corn, we waited impatiently, ready to open fire, protected against cannonfire, but hit by musketry and canister, which the enemy directed into our area. For over an hour we waited under the menacing roar of the cannons, which fired over us... The enemy were already close to our position. The skirmishers were called back from the Russbach and stepped back into the line.' (Von Ense, IR47)

Marching from Caldiero in 1813: 'The Oberst-Lt of IR63 had the first battalion advance against Waago. 1st Company dissolved into skirmish order... under the brave Hauptmann Keibel, drove the enemy back, while another part of the battalion advanced against the bridge. [They couldn't drive the enemy off it.] Hauptmann Keibel, who was steadily pushing back the enemy skirmishers ahead of him on the right... saw this [and] without waiting for orders waded through the Pronio in full view of the enemy and under their fire, to drive them off.' [On 19 October at Verona] 'both battalions formed up in front of San Martino, two divisions from the left wing remaining in companies drawn up in echelon to cover the left flank. The enemy could be seen significantly reinforcing their right wing to attack our left. Immediately, I advanced with the two companies against Madonna dela Compagnia, dissolved six Zugs into skirmish order, leaving two in reserve, with a division from IR4 as a support behind them… Supported by ferocious artillery fire, the enemy attempted to attack on his right wing with his cavalry, but I quickly gathered the skirmishers into Klumpen, and had the reserve advance.'

Despite the privations of Russia, the Austrians were victorious at Gorodetchna (11 August): two companies of Jäger and Grenzers screened a battalion of IR58 as it took the village with a battalion of IR39 in reserve. 'At the critical moment, Prince Hessen-Homburg led IR33 through the swamp above Pobbudic to help the buckling Saxon brigade. The movement was difficult: men sank to their hips, a hail of canister was fired into them. But the brave battalion under Major Porubsky reached the right side of the swamp, climbed the hills and attacked the Russian right flank. [Attacked by Russian cavalry], the battalion was steadily driven back down to the edge of the swamp. But here it was covered by 2nd Battalion, which had in the meantime reached the spot, so the regiment could hold its position… Under cover of a Battalion Mass of IR19, the brigade battery was hastily moved forward, and at the same time some companies of light troops were directed to the hills on the left [leaving] a clearly visible gap open between the two brigades. FML Bianchi ordered Major Szentvanyi with two companies of IR19 to fill the gap and advance against the hills. As this force, which carried all before it, because of its determination… appeared in the Russian left, the enemy began to buckle.'

Forming the reserve, Grenadiers were often used to assault key positions. During Leipzig in 1813 Schwarzenberg deployed 1st Brigade in three Battalion Masses on the hills to the right of the road. The two brigade batteries led the front, with skirmishers sent forward; 2nd Brigade followed and Position guns took post on the Markleeberg. Bianchi's battalions came tumbling back out, so the Call Grenadier Battalion advanced to attack Dölitz: 'It was impossible to take the village with a single assault column… [two companies] would fight their way along the river into the village and the rest of the battalion would follow slowly in support. We were successful in the first assault, carried out at the point of the bayonet.' (Hauptmann Ramberg)

In desperate close-quarters fighting, Austrian infantry storm Aspern. Fighting in small units in the villages placed a particular burden on NCO leadership. (Wöber)

Enemy reinforcements pushed them back until they were reinforced by the Fischer and Portner grenadiers. 'The village was filled with dead and wounded French and Poles, together with an enormous quantity of abandoned muskets and numerous bodies covered the fields beyond.'

Oberlt Rzieb of 3rd Battalion, IR63 described the transformation of the army since 1788:

'On 7 February 1814 at Valeggio [as enemy cavalry advanced towards our left wing], the companies were falling in; the brigade commander, GM Baron Stutterheim rode up and ordered us to form Division Masses, then to wheel to the left and march off towards the enemy; muskets were to be loaded on the march. The division of IR4 Deutschmeister marched straight ahead, those of IR3 Erzherzog Karl and IR63 Bianchi moved to the left and by this manoeuvre, the Division Masses were then brought to a halt en echequier and the battalion formed the right wing. As we drew up in this position and awaited an enemy cavalry attack, [nine Dragoon squadrons] were already moving forward at the canter, deployed and charged the enemy cavalry... After the cavalry clash had happened and there had been no shots, we thought that the enemy was only opposing us with cavalry... enemy artillery started to become audible; immediately after, musketry began and the enemy advanced in columns towards us. Enemy skirmishers were moving forward and positioning themselves in small groups behind mulberry bushes... and began to fire on our Masses, supported by several artillery pieces. Our Masses sent out skirmishers; the four guns, which were attached to the brigade, unlimbered and took up their firing positions and now there the firing was general. The enemy deployed gradually across a longer front and forced us to dissolve the Masses and deploy into open order. Because of the enemy's superior numbers and because they threatened to outflank our right, the battalion constantly had to move right, left or rearwards and then advance again. The fighting went on all day, with heavy cannonfire and musketry.'

French cavalry superiority by 1805 led the Austrians to use Masses, rapidly created by closing up columns of march. Aspern marks the end of cavalry's domination of the battlefield, as Austrian Masses felled 1,500 French cavalry. At 15 paces, the first two ranks fired devastating volleys. (von Maln)

CASUALTIES AND POWS

Mutual suffering prompted each side to help the other's wounded. An Austrian soldier moves a French officer to a casualty station by barrow at Wagram.

The later battles were characterised by heavy casualties. In Aspern village the wounded 'dragged themselves out of the houses, feeling their way along the walls, using a musket as a crutch… to the well, to the smithy… there worked a surgeon with much swearing and little skill, dead everywhere. And always fresh battalions rolled in.'

But the images were worse at Wagram: 'We lost 689 men, some of whom were brought into the first aid stations, which had been set up in the sheds of Markgrafneusiedl, and there burned alive as the enemy artillery bombarded the village. The screams of these now unarmed and immobile victims of the battle could be heard above the noise of the fighting and made my very heart freeze.' (Fähnrich Bechenie, IR4)

On campaign, field hospitals followed the army and were established on each major halt. Hospital attendants were chosen from semi-invalids and soldiers' wives, if they had no dependants and were 'not too young and attractive'. In battle, first aid stations, designated by flags, were established under the control of the Stabschirurgen (staff surgeons) behind the centre and wings and all wounded were taken there. If there were too many wounded, they were moved to the villages in the rear and treated in the field hospitals (fliegende Spitäler), being carried in empty supply wagons. These were manned by two staff surgeons and their assistants in double tents, wooden huts built by Zimmerleute, or in nearby villages. Organised by the Proto-Chirurg (Army Surgeon), sites were allocated at the last moment, often in cold wet churches, dilapidated castles, barns and cow sheds. Severely wounded were patched up and despatched to the main hospitals. Without ambulances, casualties were moved in requisitioned or spare Proviant wagons.

Rauch was hit at Valeggio (25 December 1800): 'An enemy musketball struck me in the right hip, moving past my ribs, up under the right side of my chest, where it stopped… immediately, I was grabbed under the shoulders by two of my men and carried off. The feeling… at the moment of injury was just not painful; [like] the fizzing of a hot iron thrust into cold water. Straight after, I felt a terrifying constriction in my chest, which almost took my breath away. [Having moved back] I rested a little and… allowed one of my

Most troops were moved to improvised casualty stations in nearby barns by comrades. (Seele c.1795) (BA)

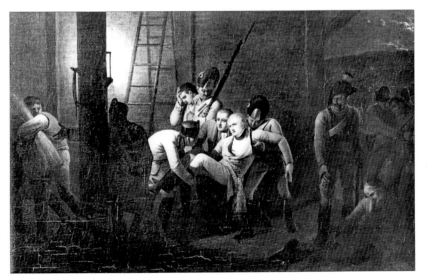

Führers to heap the powder from a live round on my wound, which he assured me would prevent it going septic.'

In the early wars, hundreds of wounded had to lie out in the open in terrible weather. The main hospitals were no better: 'The wounded lie on straw without doctors, often without any care nor the most basic food to eat, and must die there like dogs. In just two-and-a-half months the Brussels hospital alone has cost… as many men as a battle a little smaller than Neerwinden [3,000].' (Archduke Charles, 1793)

Regulations specified that officers had to be treated first at the casualty stations. Moving casualties required makeshift stretchers often carried by Sanitätstruppen (medical orderlies). (Castle)

It was no better in 1800: 'In the cold of winter, men lay on cold stones, without care. There were no doctors or regular attendants.' Charles tried to alleviate the suffering by founding four Garrison hospitals in 1808-9 and in the field, a medical cart accompanied each regiment as a first aid station. By 1812, allocated transport wagons could carry six men on straw from the first aid stations to the hospitals. Four 1,000-bed hospitals were established in Galicia with six smaller ones capable of taking 150 each.

Surgery was limited to amputation, although surgeons occasionally probed for bullets. Having reached Valeggio, Rauch dismounted at an inn, which was full of wounded. 'I begged for a drink of water – I hadn't drunk anything all day – and for the help of a doctor; for the regimental doctor had let me go to the rear unbandaged… Staff Surgeon Nobis investigated my wound; he cut into my body but soon declared he could not extract the ball without endangering my life, as I was already too exhausted… so he bandaged me with hessian – the usual bandage for the men – and, moving away, told me to be courageous and rest.'

Bound by their regulations not to maltreat prisoners, this rule was not always reciprocated. Two battalions of IR4 captured at Landrecy in 1794 found themselves confined 'in dreadful conditions in churches, abandoned sheds and animal stalls. They lay on the bare earth… exposed to the hardships of a hard winter, as these quarters couldn't be heated and the uniforms had deteriorated to such an extent, that they hardly covered these wretches… all lacked overcoats and shoes. A bucket of water was pushed under the door, which was filled with water once a day – no-one was allowed to leave the quarters to relieve himself… Small groups escaped and reached the border travelling along tracks by night… All these brave troops lacked shoes, disfigured by the misery and dangers they had overcome.' Of those captured, 500 were never seen again.

Although during the siege of Genoa in 1800, Massena allowed several thousand prisoners to starve to death on prison hulks, Napoleon improved their treatment. POWs returning from the War of the Second

Local Viennese interring Austrian and French bodies after Wagram. Most were burned and placed in local church crypts. (BA)

Coalition reported that they had been 'treated quite well, receiving daily, 50 Sous [French small currency] for Hauptleute, Oberlts 38, Unterlts and Fähnrichs 27, Feldwebels 8, Korporals 6, Gefreite 4, Gemeine 3... the men were held in something akin to barracks and were even provided with bread.'

Some French prisoners were marched as far as Pest and eastern fortresses, but increasingly both sides released troops on parole, agreeing not to serve again for a year and a day. Prisoner exchanges were frequently negotiated, with large numbers returning to the army. Rzieb took 400 from various regiments to Moravia to re-equip them and return them to the army at Wagram. However, French setbacks in 1813 led them to starve Austrian POWs captured at Dresden in order to force them to enlist.

Returning home, Austria's victorious soldiers were offered a different field implement in 1815. (Castle)

AFTERMATH

Victorious at Aspern, one officer reflected upon priorities: 'During the three days of fighting, hunger had really made itself felt, but after the battle, it was sleep that was more necessary.' Retreat after Wagram brought additional hardship: 'The tragic remains of our brave regiment [IR49]... fell back to Bockfliess, where we only rested for a few minutes, so that we could obtain fresh water, for despite the heavy rains [during the night of 4/5 July], the heat of [5 July] had been so great that there were no puddles; our tongues stuck to our lips and, as we hadn't eaten for 48 hours, hunger began to torment us.'

If the army withdrew, wounded were left to their own devices. Viennese civilians went out to that battlefield to tend the wounded of both sides. Many Austrians, consumed by searing fever, begged French troops to bayonet them. Some cursed the French, but most accepted water. Following Austerlitz, wounded dragged themselves to French bivouac fires to escape the cold. Men who had fought each other hours before sat together round the fires.

Now the effects of battle set in. Fähnrich Baron Bechenie of IR4 had fought his first action at Wagram: 'I wish that I was still sitting on the bench in the Neustadt Academy... today, I know nothing except that I am still holding the flag in my hand... Lt Baron Bessler asked me what I felt about this painful retreat. I merely shook my head.'

Retreat would damage the army's cohesion. After Dresden (26 August 1813), Major Zagitschek of IR15 wrote: 'As the rain had fallen in torrents for several days, the night march through the Tharandter Forest, where we were often up to our hips in water, was particularly difficult; the men completely soaked through, exhausted by the bad road, often became separated, which caused considerable disorder. On deploying in our position, we looked dreadful... We had not eaten for 24 hours, the Proviant wagons being unable to keep up. The roads were unmade, the army had already stripped everything there was from every village. Stragglers plundered the houses and mistreated local people... every man was concerned for himself and thanked his comrade for a piece of bread or a raw turnip, when they could be obtained. For two days, I lived on raw turnips, which were found by the men in the fields.' Other men ran off into the woods and could only be reassembled by blowing horns.'

Musket stock blanks with locks. (Castle)

The end of a campaign took the troops back to their garrisons. Those who were unfit were placed in 3rd Battalions; those with one eye, or afflictions such as stiffness, withering of limbs or scrofula, were designated 'half-invalid' and joined the Garrison or Cordon (searching out deserters) Battalions. Soldiers were only invalided out on strict criteria, certified by army doctors; often they remained in the regiment as officers' servants or medical orderlies.

Bullet moulds created a ball with an extra lump, which could be tied to the cartridge. (Castle)

Alternatively, they could leave with 50 Gulden or enter one of the Invalid Houses, which accommodated 220 officers and 3,670 men, paid and receiving bread at just below peacetime rates. The literate could take recruitment or administrative jobs, and fitter men were encouraged to set up in trade.

A Sterquartel (3 months' pay) was paid to any widow or children, or if there were no children, to the invalid fund. Post-1802 soldiers finishing their Capitulation received a grant. (see table below.)

Twenty-four years of hostilities ended in 1815. IR4 Deutschmeister had fought 90 actions against the French, losing nearly 200 officers and over 5,000 men. The distress continued for some, including 'Unterleutnant Nemeth, whom his French captors had thrust into a fire in 1815 and who had, as a consequence, lost his left eye, his nose and a part of his upper lip. He was rewarded for his pains with an annual pension of 200 Gulden'.

Hamstrung by politicians, finances and shortages, the victors of Neerwinden, Würzburg, Novi, Stockach, Aspern and Leipzig carried the

1814 regimental band. After fifers were abolished in 1806, the bands were regulated at 10 Hautboisten and up to 38 Bandisten, who played the popular 'Turkish music' on instruments including the Schellenbaum (centre) and the large drum (right). (Umhey Collection)

burden of Continental fighting, impressing Napoleon in defeat at Marengo and Wagram. One officer questioned whether an army of 'Hungarians, Croats, Transylvanians, Italians, Bohemians, Moravians, Poles, Vlachs, Slovenians, Austrians, Styrians, Carnioleans and gypsies could march under one flag and fight for a cause it knows nothing about'. It is remarkable that they did.

Already unformed, IR31 storm the burning church at Aspern. Several men wear their greatcoats across their bodies to protect against sabre blows.

	Up to 6 years	More than 6 years
Feldwebel	6 Gulden	10 Gulden
Korporal	4 Gulden	7 Gulden
Gefreiter	2 Gu 30 kr	4 Gulden

THE PLATES

A: 1788-98 INFANTRYMAN

This man is wearing the 1769 pattern uniform with his backpack on a 32 Zoll long and one Zoll wide belt slung over the shoulder. The 16cm high Kaskett was made of leather with some felt. Few had the 1779 leather peak. Firing a lead ball weighing 26g, the beech musket was to be stained black at the regiment's expense. The number of patterns introduced meant that during the Revolutionary Wars, up to three were used within a company. The barrel had to be thick enough to sustain firing a double charge. In bad weather the misfire rate reached 50%, so soldiers used leather lock covers, canvas gun bags and a barrel cork. **1** The Okonomie Regulation of 1773 prescribed a leather cartridge box, carrying 36 rounds and six canister rounds. It measured 32cm x 24cm and was hung on a 10cm wide bandoleer. **2** Brass cartridge box badge, issued until 1798, although still in use beyond 1809. **3** 1780 Giradoni Air rifle. **4** Air rifle lock mechanism. **5** 1769 Granatgewehr – carried by Infanterie-Arkebusiers. The two-and-a-half pound grenade had to be loaded with the fuse up against the powder charge, the strong kick ameliorated by a recoil hook. **6** 1754 Commissflinte – 6/4 Löth calibre (18.3mm) with 1748 bayonet. **7** 1767 musket with a 1767 bayonet secured by a hook. **8** 1767 swan-neck lock. **9** 1784 pattern musket, based on Prussian self-loading designs with a deeper pan and brass flashguard. **10** 1784 pattern lock. **11** Fusilier sabre 1765 with 53cm blade. **12** Detail of fusilier sabre 1784. **13** 6/4 Löth canister round, comprising three to four small balls (total weight: 26g).

B: 1788-91 THE TURKISH WARS

The primary defence against Turkish cavalry was the late 17th century Spanischer Reiter. Used mainly in camps, on the flanks and with detachments, every 31cm there was a hole bored through to accommodate the Schweinfeder, measuring 180cm. A detachment of 25 men, each armed with a musket and Schweinfeder, were equipped with a beam (10cm x 10cm x 371cm), carried by two men alternately. The Reiter were also used in creating bridgeheads over the Save in June 1789. The bridge was thrown, and the Reiter was carried over and placed along the outer edges, so the pioneers could construct the bridgehead within them.

1788 Wagenburgen (see diagram over): 'The soldiers always camped, if not in square, then depending on the terrain, in a closed-up formation, behind which were the Wagenburgen.' In 1812 Schwarzenberg revived Wagenburgen to fend off Russian cavalry in the open, although smaller and without Reiter. 'Once the Korps has completed its concentration, then the transports…are to form up in Wagenburgen [commanded by an officer]. The transports and baggage of each infantry division are to form up in a single Wagenburg behind their respective second line, the lines parallel to it to be twice the length of the side lines. Part of the horses are to be harnessed on the shafts and the rest in the inner area.' One company formed a reserve against cavalry attack. On the march, the Burgen were to be protected with flank patrols and if enemy cavalry were sighted, the wagons were to form into small Burgen depending on the terrain, where the infantry patrols would join them.

C: 1798-1810 INFANTRYMAN

He is wearing the 1798 uniform and hairstyle, five Zoll long with four bound. Helmets were phased out from 1806 on

Wagenburg c. 1788

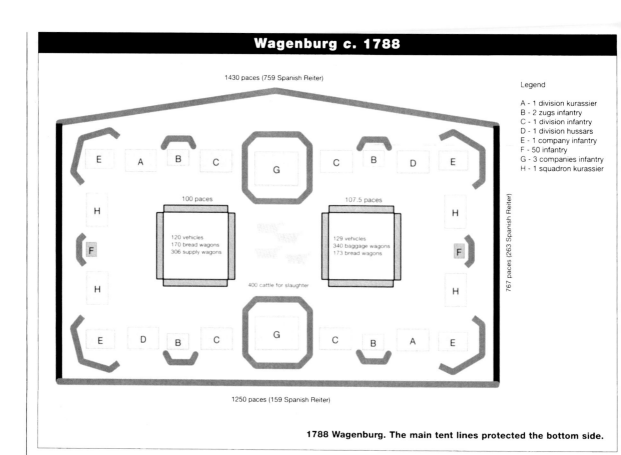

1788 Wagenburg. The main tent lines protected the bottom side.

(Legend)

A - 1 division kurassier
B - 2 zugs infantry
C - 1 division infantry
D - 1 division hussars
E - 1 company infantry
F - 50 infantry
G - 3 companies infantry
H - 1 squadron kurassier

1430 paces (759 Spanish Reiter)

100 paces
120 vehicles
170 bread wagons
306 supply wagons

107.5 paces
129 vehicles
340 baggage wagons
173 bread wagons

400 cattle for slaughter

767 paces (263 Spanish Reiter)

1250 paces (159 Spanish Reiter)

---

grounds of cost and weight, many becoming unwearable with head wounds.

1 1807 cooking pot with separate lid, doubling as a frying pan. **2** 5/4 Löth calibre 1798 musket, based on the French 1777 pattern. Introduced over 10 years, it fired a 21.5g ball and its brass mountings were easier to clean. **3** 1798 lock. Galician 'Podolische Feuersteine' were suitable flints for the heavier locks. The stone was supplied with a lead casing, making it easier to change in battle (leather covers were substituted). After misfires, the stone could be 'knapped', sharpening the edge with musket tools. A stone lasted about 25 shots – a good one lasted 50. Ammunition wagons carried 5,000 flints in small barrels or 19,000 in powder barrels. Once empty, the barrels were used for target shooting. During the Revolutionary Wars Austria consumed 50 million stones. **4** 1807 musket – a copy of the 1798, except that it was plain wood with iron mountings. **5** Officer's 1809 pistol: small version of the 1798 lock, made of walnut. **6** 1798 5/4 Löth round. **7** 5/4 Löth drill round. **8** Made from captured cannon, the 1814 Kannonkreuz was the first general service medal. Recipients could put their names on the reverse. **9** Hungarian boots and German shoes. Footwear had to be changed daily for even wear: the thick leather was smeared with wax to prevent water penetration. **10** 1798 cartridge box on a 10cm bandoleer. Each soldier was issued with three or four spare flints carried in a small leather bag under the cartridge box lid. Infantry carried 60 rounds with 40 shots per weapon in the first reserve. **11** 1773 metal waterbottle with white leather strap. **12** 1798 pattern lock (cutaway).

D: HUNGARIAN RECRUITMENT 1811

'I do not entertain the hope always to be able to keep the Hungarian regiments up to full complement with just volunteers' (Archduke Charles). To find 'volunteers', recruitment parties would take performers dressed in elaborate clothes to dance at local fairs. 'They started with slow and measured steps and it then became more energetic. The performers would clap their hands, slap them on their boots and then bring their heels sharply together until...the peasants became enthusiastic and joined in...the soldiers would add something for the sake of effect...not ceasing until their spurs are shattered and...overcome by fatigue.' Enthusiastic peasants would be invited to volunteer and soon found themselves being marched off. Another ruse shown here involved a gypsy band, lots of wine and girls. Stopping in the marketplaces, the gypsies played, the wine was free and girls with shakos on their heads invited the boys to dance. If, while dancing, the girl was able to put the shako on the boy's head, he was considered a volunteer. In his holiday clothes, this Slavonian peasant from the Neutra district, home of IR2, is about to join up courtesy of a local peasant girl. Anyone objecting was swiftly manacled and marched away.

E: RECRUITS FIRING MUSKETS
(1806 ABRICHTUNGSREGLEMENT S. 4)

A *Spannt den Hahn!* – The right thumb pulls the hammer until there is a click signifying it is at half-cock. *Ergreift die*

Patrone! – The right hand takes the cartridge from its box, the ball alongside the small finger. The cartridge was bitten at the top of the powder.

B *Pulver auf die Pfanne!* – Powder was poured into the pan to level. *Schliesst die Pfanne!* – The frizzen is closed with the last two fingers. *Schwenkt zur Ladung!* – The weapon was placed on the ground by the left shoe toe and held off-vertical.

C *Patrone in Lauf!* – The powder is shaken out of the cartridge into the barrel. The ball is pressed in with the thumb and index finger. *Ladstock in Lauf!* – The ramrod is drawn out as far as the right arm will reach, then grasped again and completely removed. Without turning it, the ramrod is pushed two Zoll into the barrel, then the arm is fully extended and the ramrod driven into the barrel. *Setzt an, versorgt den Ladstock!* – An extra push with the ramrod, which then is snapped quickly out of the barrel with the arm fully extended, and dropped back into its rings, giving a short strike with the flat of the hand.

D Once proficient, firing drill was conducted. *Pton!* (Subunit!) – The soldier faced his front moving the musket to the Present position. *Fert!* (Ready!) – The right hand grips the neck of the butt and the thumb pulls the hammer back to full cock. *An!* (Take aim!) – The soldier turned right, moving his right foot one Fuss behind his left. The weapon was moved sharply to the horizontal position and the index finger inside the trigger guard. The butt was pressed into the shoulder; the left eye closed and the right looking along the barrel, sight and the line of aim. *Feuer!* (Fire!) If the round had fired, the touchhole was smoking. If the touchhole was blocked, the recruit was instructed to clear it with the touchhole pin. In action, the sequence was *Fert, An, Feuer!* until the command *Setzt ab!* (cease firing). Drills were conducted with wooden cartridges of the same length as a live round. Hornstone (impure flint) was inserted into the hammer, and was blunted on the front edge to avoid damaging the frizzen. For target practice, a sand-filled barrel with three black targets representing the head, chest and lower body was placed at a height of six Schuh. The soldier was taught to aim at the target's chest, at varying distances of 150, 200-250 and 300 paces.

F: 'YOU DID NOT SEE THE AUSTRIANS AT (ASPERN-)ESSLING; THEREFORE YOU HAVE NOT SEEN ANYTHING' (NAPOLEON)

Some of the worst fighting of the wars happened in Aspern village. Small groups of soldiers defended each house like a small fortress, unable to see far in the smoke. 'There was fighting in every alley, in every house and in every shed; wagons, ploughs, harrows had to be dragged out of the way under unceasing fire in order to get to hand-to-hand fighting with the enemy. Every single wall was an obstacle for the attacker and a defensive position for the defender…holding the village wasn't possible for long, for hardly had we taken an alley or house, than the enemy stormed another and forced us to abandon the first.' (*Kreig 1809*, Vol. 4)

The church was bitterly contested. 'We stormed the cemetery and immediately drove the French out. Hardly had we taken up position in it, when a new French force attacked us and chased us back out. Over this [four-foot-high] wall my comrades sought safety in flight. I was however too small

and incapable of getting over in my heavy kit. The noise and confusion was dreadful; the French were right behind us with their bayonets. I believed I was lost, when a Bohemian chap grabbed me round the chest, dragged me up into the air and threw me over the wall…one moment later and I would have been captured or killed.' (Fähnrich Höpler of IR47)

G: HUNGARIAN GRENADIER AND ZIMMERMAN (PIONEER) 1798-1816

'Among the Austrian uniforms, the Hungarian Grenadiers provided a marvellous sight.' In their 32cm bearskins Hungarian Grenadiers were 'seen' as often as the Imperial Guard; at Eggmühl (where they weren't) and at Marengo (just three of Latterman's five battalions). **A** The Zimmerman wears the 1811 shako. **1** Axe and Zelthacke. **2** Axe carrying cases. **3** Zimmerman's apron. **B** The Grenadier wears the post-1801 bearskin with peak and side flaps. His hair is one Zoll overall, decreed on 30 July 1805. **4** Match case. **5** Grenade badge, worn on the cartridge box and from 1811 on the cross belt. **6** 1777 sabre. **7** 1802 iron-mounted sabre. **8-9** 1769 backpack. **10** 1771 Infantry Zelthacke, carried in the pouch on the backpack. **11** Old-style wooden water bottle. Both these last items officially were only carried by every second man.

H: HUNGARIAN GRENADIERS AT WÜRZBURG 3 SEPTEMBER 1796

Advancing at *ordinär* pace, using a looser form of the 1769 regulation requirement for 'toes pointed somewhat outwards. Both knees are to be held stiff and the feet raised only as for normal walking and not stamped when they come down'. As required, the '[r]ight arm hangs naturally at the side, the left arm holds the musket with the butt in the hand…the arm only bent so far that the gun can be turned and immediately grasped by the right hand on the neck with the right arm horizontal.'

The Reserve Division (GM Werneck's 12 Grenadier battalions) reached Bibergau around 3 pm to replace the cavalry previously shoring up Sztaray's right, so that they could attack the French. As the French retreated, the Austrians began a general advance northwest along the entire front at 4pm. Werneck's Grenadiers were ordered to clear the Rotenhof area to secure the links between Sztaray's division and Wartensleben's Reserve cavalry. Three Grenadier battalions attacked Rotenhof under heavy canister fire, but released the 2nd Slavonian Grenzer battalion and O'Donnel Freikorps to move up into the wooded hills beyond.

I: THEY WENT TO RUSSIA TOO 1812

The troops were poorly clothed. Many were marching barefoot by the end of September, so Schwarzenberg allowed them to make Opanken (Balkan footwear) from the Schlachtvieh hides. The lack of greatcoats meant that by mid-October every two men had to be given a piece of sheepskin to protect at least the lower body and head against the cold. One eyewitness, Weiden, wrote: 'If anyone was so fortunate, in addition to his [basic needs] to capture some loot, or discover a store of potatoes, or even buried bottles of brandy, then he would have an especially good night.' The soldiers did not discuss pay, precisely because there was nothing to buy, but the total lack of bread, biscuit, wine, tobacco and salt was desperate. The army commissariat 'only succeeded in supplying bread every 8-14 days. There was no talk of uniforms or shoes...the daily marches and bivouacs were accompanied by all the shortages. These steadily increased and no overnight camp was left without several dead, who had suffered miserably, being buried.' (The Commissariat Chief died of the strain in February 1813.)

J: 1807 BATTALION SKIRMISHING
(1807 EXERCIERREGLEMENT)

The 1807 Regulations provided training for skirmishing. Although all troops were drilled, the best troops needed 'particular ability in using their weapon, physical agility, steadiness, judgement, cunning and self-belief'. Alongside sharpshooting, he had to be able to load while sitting, kneeling and moving. Then the skirmisher was taught to use local terrain, vegetation and even dung heaps to his advantage. If attacked by enemy cavalry, he was to fire at close range and then use his bayonet against the rider's left side or the horse's chest.

60-80 skirmishers would screen a battalion. Moving at *dublir* from the third line, three large Zugs would move up, half of each controlled by three NCOs forming their sector of the screen up to 300 paces from the main line. Working in groups of two or three, they used local features as cover within a few paces of the screen line. 80-100 paces back came the other half of each Zug as the supports, closed up in two lines. Another 100 paces back were the other three Zugs of the reserves, each commanded by a Hauptmann. Troops were rotated through the screen from the supports, half a Zug at a time, spreading into a single line to replace those in front. Leaving the screen without permission brought instant execution.

Drum signals from the battalion command were repeated by the drummer alongside each Hauptmann in the reserves. In a withdrawal, the screen pulled back alternately in two lines, 10 paces at a time, the supports moving back 20-30 paces when the screen came within 50. Once the screen was 200 paces from the main line, it turned about and moved back at *dublir*, then faced its front. If the skirmish units were under threat, they cleared the front and re-formed on the wings, firing on the enemy flanks, while the main line received the enemy with volleys and canister.

K: BATTALION AND DIVISION MASSES
(1807 EXERCIERREGLEMENT)

As the troops loaded, the officers on the sides ordered the four flank files to turn to each side. To protect the vulnerable corners, these files could aim obliquely. *At Fert!* – The first four ranks brought their weapons into position; the others remained with shouldered weapons. *Erstes Glied, fällt das Bajonnet!* (Front rank, lower bayonets!) – with the butt held against the crook of the elbow. The second rank opened fire when enemy cavalry reached 300 paces. *Zweites Glied, An! Feuer!* – Their muskets were then brought to the vertical and quickly exchanged for the loaded musket of the third rank. A second volley was immediately fired by the second rank, who then lowered their weapons as for the first. As the enemy reached 50-60 paces, from the lowered position; *Erstes Glied, Feuer!*

As the second rank fired, the third exchanged the discharged weapons for the fourth rank's muskets. If the enemy risked close-quarters action, the first rank used their bayonets on the horses, the second on the cavalrymen. The third rank fired their weapons at the enemy's upper body, singling out the bravest troopers (reducing the danger to the forward ranks). If the three ranks had fired, then all four ranks immediately reloaded and continued until the drums beat 'cease fire'.

Unlike Waterloo, the Austrians faced an all-arms assault at Aspern. Formed up *en echequier* 250 feet apart, with about 60 paces in between, the closed-up Masses created a killing zone, as French cavalry flowed through. Smoke reduced ranges and concentrated fire. The second rank fired at 100 paces. At Wagram, French cavalryman Parquin saw 'at 100 paces, a terrible volley...cause the most fearful confusion'. It killed one general, several officers and over 50 troopers. Then, fire was held by both ranks until 10-15 paces for maximum effect. Needing to extend the battle line, regiments deployed in Division Mass to maintain the frontage, while offering a shallower artillery target. Not shown here, artillery pieces located between the Masses would fire canister with each volley.

If skirmishers approached, men were despatched from the sixth row of the front and rear sides or from the fourth side ranks to drive them off. They didn't venture far, so that they could return at *dublir* without disordering the Mass. Alternatively, sharpshooters within each Zug fired on them. If caught in the open or a Mass broke up, troops could gather around an NCO in Klumpen of two circular ranks with bayonets lowered.

L: GRENADIERS AND INFANTRY IN CAMP
AROUND 1811

The Sanität (medical orderly) soldier's 1809 uniform was similar to the 1813 Landwehr with 'S.C.' on the Corsehut shield. In the background is a Feldschmeide.

Literacy levels prompted the *Verhaltungen aus dem Kompagnie-Reglement der k.k. Österreichischen Armee in Fragen und Antworten* in 1808, a question and answer booklet used by NCOs to test the men on the key regulations. One soldier's answers to questions about cleaning his musket reveal the variety of geology in his backpack. 109: How must a soldier keep his iron-work clean? This must be kept rust free and cleaned with fine hematite or magnetite. 110: How is the brasswork to be maintained? With Rottenstone (silicate limestone). 112: Should the musket's lock mechanism be rubbed with hematite? No, but it should only occasionally be rubbed with Binsenstein (more limestone) and then washed off. 116: How should the lock mechanism be treated, so that it remains in working order and rust-free? It must be frequently dampened with olive oil, as well as all the screws in their holes and even the shaft of the musket as well. Having observed 115: Is it permitted to clean the barrel with the ramrod? No, because it causes damage. The task was completed with 117: What is to be done when the oil has penetrated? Then everything can be wiped down cleanly with a piece of cloth.

His food is cooking in a 1771 Feldkochgeschinirr, which weighed 3.71kg and served the needs of four men. Each regiment's camp had four small white square 'camp flags', bearing the regimental number. They were edged officially in Madder red, but were often in the facing colour.

BIBLIOGRAPHY

Coverage of the Austrian Army in English has greatly improved recently. The key works remain: G. Rothenburg, *Napoleon's Great Adversary: Archduke Charles and the Austrian Army* (rep. 1995) and C. Duffy, *The Army of Maria Theresa 1740-80* (rep. 1990). There are many drill diagrams and related information in G. Nafziger, *Imperial Bayonets* (1996), although the Geschwindschritt is wrongly calculated. There are regular items in the magazine *Age of Napoleon* (Partizan Press, UK). Many battles will be covered in the Helmet Feldzug Series (B. Voykowitsch, Vienna).

As well as the original regulations, useful German references include: *Oesterreichische Militaer Almanach* (1790-1803) and *Schematis der kk Armee (1804-1815)*; the three series of the *Mitteilungen des Kriegsarchivs (1881-1914)*; Wrede: *Supplement zur Mitteilungen des Kriegsarchivs* (5 vols); the Staff histories *Kriege gegen die Französische Revolution, Krieg 1809* and *Befreiungskriege 1813-14*, and J Gallina, *Beiträge zur Geschichte des österreichischen Heerwesens (1872)*. On weaponry and kit – Krenn, *Die Handfeuerwaffen des österreichischen Soldaten (Graz Exhibition 1985)*; Dolleczek, *Monographie der k.u.k. österrung. blanken und Handfeuer-Waffen (rep. 1970)*; and Rivista Militaire, *The Last Soldiers of the Holy Roman Empire*. The Okonomie drawings of 1771 comprise most early equipment and uniforms.

Printed memoirs are rare, but include A. Ellrich (Ed) *Humoristische und historische Skizzen aus den Jahren der Revolutionskriege. Aus den hinterlassenen Papieren eines verstorbenen Soldaten* (Mandelham) (Meissen 1844); J Rauch, *Erinnerungen eines Offiziers aus Altösterreich*: Vol.21 of A. Weber, *Denkwürdigkeiten aus Altösterreich* (Munich 1918); and C. Varnhagen von Ense, *Die Schlacht von Wagram 1809* (1836). Other useful references include: Allmayer-Beck/Lessing, *Das Heer unter dem Doppeladler 1718-1848* (1978); F. Wöber, *1809: Schlacht bei Aspern und Essling* (1992) and the *Militärhistorische Schriftenreihe* series.

Collections are held in: the Heeresgeschichtliches Museum, near the Sudbahnhof, Vienna; Hadtoetenet Intezet es Muzeum at Toth Arpadsetany, Budapest; and the Museum of Military History in the former Schwarzenberg Palace, Prague. The main weaponry collection is in the Landeszeughaus in Graz, and large supplies of equipment have survived in the former depot at Castle Forchtenstein in the Burgenland. Many Austrian provincial museums have small collections of local finds. Vast numbers of unresearched documents are held in the Vienna Kriegsarchiv and the Budapest State Archives.

Multi-national Austrian re-enactors (Waterloo 1995): IR2 Tsar of Russia Grenadiers (Slovakia); 2nd Battalion IR4 Deutschmeister (UK); IR1 Kaiser Grenadiers (Czech Republic); IR20 Kaunitz (Czech Republic); IR56 W. Colloredo (Italy). Other units portray: Artillery (Czech Republic); IR44 Belgiojoso (Italy); 1es Jäger (UK/Austria); Hussars (Hungary).

INDEX

(References to illustrations are shown in **bold**. Plates are shown with commentary locators in brackets).